Writing for Public Relations

by George A. Douglas

Emerson College, Boston

Charles E. Merrill Publishing Co.
A Bell & Howell Company
Columbus   Toronto   London   Sydney

To my father,
the late George A. Douglas,
the ultimate teacher.

Published by Charles E. Merrill Publishing Co.
A Bell & Howell Company
Columbus, Ohio 43216

This book was set in Optima.
Production Editor: Jan Hall
Cover Design Coordination: Will Chenoweth

Library of Congress Catalog Card Number: 79–90026

International Standard Book Number: 0–675–08171–8

Printed in the United States of America

4 5 6 7 8 9 10—85 84 83

Preface

Communications is the lifeblood of public relations. A practitioner must be competent in a variety of writing assignments: news releases, brochure copy, institutional advertising, speeches, annual reports, documentary films, and answering complaint letters.

The problem is that he or she may do one type of writing frequently while attempting another only on a rare occasion.

This book is written with this problem in mind, taking each writing responsibility step by step: the prewriting considerations, the problems that might be encountered, and examples of the specific assignment.

Writing for Public Relations is a balance between theory and example.

Contents

2
The news release and its use in the media   17

3
Brochures, pamphlets, and booklets   27

4
The annual report   39

5
Public relations and institutional advertising   59

6
Speech writing   75

7
Visuals   97

8
The company publication   119

9
Newsletters   141

Overview

Today's public relations practitioner employs many communication and administrative skills. Depending on the needs of the organization he serves, he may assume the multiple roles of administrator, counselor, researcher, and spokesperson. At times he may hire specialists in certain communication fields, but he must himself possess two basic abilities:

1. To listen, observe, and interpret public opinion, and

2. To write concisely and persuasively.

The practitioner uses these skills to formulate and carry out a public relations strategy. The strategy involves several steps, each ongoing and of equal importance:

1. *Research*—discover the public's attitudes.

2. *Planning*—chart the strategy and its course.

3. *Communication*—tell the public.

4. *Evaluation*—find out the program's effectiveness.

Each of these steps directly involves the public relations practitioner. Throughout this book, public relations strategy and the skills of the practitioner as listener and writer will be examined carefully in many different aspects.

In the first two chapters, the news release is presented as a vital tool to the practitioner. These chapters detail the basics about writing releases and the factors behind an editor's judgment on when to use a release.

Sometimes, however, the mass media cannot reach a special public. Chapter 3 proposes a solution to this problem, explaining how to write brochures, pamphlets, or booklets in a nonjournalistic style. In addition, Chapter 4 shows how the annual report can be useful to both profit and nonprofit organizations. The writing style of the report must be precise—the appearance of the report reflects the personality of the management, whether progressive, conservative, or middle-of-the-road.

The next chapter, 5, discusses all facets of institutional advertising, including how to write persuasive copy for both print and broadcast.

Because speech writing is a frequent public relations assignment, Chapter 6 provides information on special approaches to certain types of speeches.

Although the public relations practitioner is not a film technician, he will sometimes be asked to produce a program with visuals. Chapter 7 discusses how to merge visuals with a script and the processes behind films and slide presentations.

The remainder of the text speaks to specific concerns of the practitioner. Chapter 8 shows how the practitioner's writing skills make the company publication effective in strengthening employee morale and productivity. Chapter 9 illustrates how newsletters can be used to communicate with a special public. How to write position papers (used in lobbying) and how to answer complaint letters are the topics of Chapters 10 and 11, respectively. Finally, although fund raising is usually not the practitioner's responsibility, Chapter 12 presents guidelines for producing fund-raising literature for nonprofit organizations.

1

The news release

A good news release reaches the public economically and efficiently, informing everyone of an event. However, some public relations practitioners who do not have training or experience in journalism find it hard to write a good release. Their sentences are too long, their story's content confusing, and their leads misleading. An editor who can't figure out these kinds of releases ignores them; he has hundreds of other stories on his desk that are clear and concise.

The professional practitioner not only writes clearly; he also delivers the release to the media in ample time, allowing the editor or reporter to rewrite, edit, or even obtain more information if needed. No news release, no matter how relevant, will be used if received too late.

The lead

The first paragraph of the story, called the *lead,* is the most important part of the piece. It introduces the story, tells what it is about and actually is a synopsis of the story.

The lead sentence usually runs longer than the other sentences in the release. It may total thirty words, three typewritten lines. Most news writers feel that a four-line lead (forty words) is too long.

Elements of the lead

Traditionally, news writers follow the "five *W*'s and an *H*" in lead writing (*who, what, where, when, why,* and *how*). However, use of all these elements could produce a sentence that is too long and cumbersome. Which to include in the lead depends on the specific need of the story. For example:

> Three Brighton residents have been elected officers of the City Savings Bank, John F. Ellis, president, announced today.

In this illustration, the lead is short, a total of nineteen words. It answers *who, what, when,* and *where*:

1. *Who*: three Brighton residents
2. *What*: their election as officers
3. *Where*: the City Savings Bank
4. *When*: today

Notice that *why* and *how* are not needed in the lead. Instead, *how* is answered in the second paragraph:

> Marion B. Bennett, Robert H. Jordan, and James P. Mullins were elected loan officers at the Board of Directors' meeting.

The remainder of the release contains the educational, career, and family backgrounds of the newly elected officers. *Why* is not needed in the lead or in the story at all.

In most news releases, *who* is a person, organization, company, or community. It should appear in the lead almost without exception. For example:

> The president of State University today banned motorcycles on campus.

1. *Who* is the president of State University. His name isn't important; he's identified as the president and there is no confusion as to who he is.

2. *Where* is the location of the event or action and usually occurs in leads. In this example, *where* is the campus.

3. *What* refers to the happening or occurrence; it's the reason that the story was written. In this lead, *what* is the banning of motorcycles.

4. *When* plays an important role in the lead because the time element of most news stories is paramount. How tight the time element of a news story is (*today, yesterday, last week*) depends on the story and the medium it appears in. In this lead, *when* is today.

5. *Why* refers to the cause, reason, or purpose of the event. In some stories, *why* is an important part of the lead. But in this example, the college's public relations practitioner felt that the action (the banning of motorcycles) was the lead's feature. Another person might consider *why* important and write this lead:

   > Death of a student last week in a tragic accident resulted in the University president's decision today to ban the use of motorcycles on campus.

6. *How* is not used in either leads, because it is not needed. But it is a basic element in other stories, especially those in which there is something important about how the event occurred. For example:

   > Four senior members were elected to the Executive Council of the Board of Directors yesterday after three junior members withdrew from the election.

In this lead, one can ask, "How were the senior members elected?" The answer is clear: when the three junior members withdrew.

Writing a lead becomes easier with experience. Rewrite it as many times as necessary to tell the story concisely and comprehensively. Time spent is well worth the investment. Finally, ask yourself this question: *Will it stand on its own as a one-paragraph story?*

Thus you can see that as far as the "five W's and an H" rule is concerned, each news release must be written on its own merits.

"Say-nothing" and "say-everything" leads

An inexperienced writer can fall into two traps: the "say-nothing" or the "say-everything" lead. Each spells doom for the release; the editor chucks these leads into the wastebasket. For example, here's a "say-nothing" lead:

> The YGA Corporation held its annual meeting at the corporation headquarters in Huntville yesterday and stockholders voted on a number of vital questions.

There is no real news in the lead—all we learn is that a meeting was held. The editor throws the release away in frustration.

Also frustrating is the lead trying to say everything:

> The YGA Corporation held its annual meeting at the corporation headquarters in Huntville yesterday, with the re-election of George C. Owens as chief executive officer, who announced an excellent year for the corporation, resulting in an expansion program, which would include construction of a plant employing 200 new workers, including men and women.

This story tells something newsworthy—the construction of a plant with the hiring of 200 new workers. However, it took the editor seven lines of copy to find the real news hidden away. A more workable lead would be:

> Two hundred new jobs with the construction of a plant was announced yesterday at the annual stockholders' meeting of the YGA Corporation in Huntville.

This lead focuses on what is important to the local residents: the jobs. Thus, while the "say-nothing lead" fails to relate any information, the "say-everything" lead says too much, confusing the reader with trivia mixed with important facts. Because the goal of any lead is to satisfy the reader's desire for immediate information, the essential elements are at the beginning:

Two hundred new jobs;
Motorcycles banned on campus;
Three Brighton residents elected officers.

The body

News writers traditionally structure stories in an inverted pyramid form. In this form, the important elements are at the upper, wide end of the pyramid; the less important information falls to the lower part. This structure allows the reader to glance at the lead and understand the story. He can decide whether or not to continue reading; he already has a synopsis of the story. Additionally, an editor with a space problem on a page can cut off the last paragraphs and not harm the story's continuity because the vital facts are at the top. (See Figure 1–1.)

News item order

News releases offer the facts in the order of their news value, not according to their chronological order. For example, the executive committee of a religious group votes on five resolutions taking a public stand on various issues. The recording secretary, in writing the minutes of the meeting, reports on resolution one, two, and three as each resolution is voted on by the members. After the meeting, the practitioner leads his story with resolution three because it has news value while the others do not have significance for the general public.

> The anti-abortion forces of the First Church won yesterday when the Executive Committee voted to take a public stand against a state bill permitting legal abortions.
> The vote was unanimous among the 40 committee members at their regular monthly meeting. The stand against legalizing abortions in this state was voted on after a bitter debate between the pro-abortion wing of the church and the "right-to-life" group.

Unified stories

When an effective news release is unified, each fact relates to the specific focus of the story. Sentences and paragraphs tie together smoothly; the

NEWS RELEASE:

   10 FORBES ROAD, BRAINTREE, MA 02184 (617) 848-7380

Please contact:
Marion King
Nights: 967 8090

IMMEDIATE RELEASE

Insufficient exercise is a major cause of low
back pain among adult Americans, Rosemarie Knickles, director of
exercise at Gloria Stevens Figure Salons, states.

Sedentary lifestyles led by most Americans
cause improper muscular development, Ms. Knickles said. The larger
muscle groups are not used enough causing a lack of sufficient
strength for proper body alignment, she added.

Weak abdominal muscles cause the pelvis to
drop down in front, Ms. Knickles said. This puts pressure on the
spine in the lower back and causes a backache.

Tight muscles at the back of the thighs
(hamstrings) caused by continual sitting create pain upon standing,
Ms. Knickles revealed.

Most people who suffer from low back pain
can alleviate the problem by exercising regularly, she said.
She warned that the selection of the proper exercises is important.

Exercises which strengthen the abdominal
muscles and stretch those at the back of the thighs should be
selected, Ms. Knickles added.

=end=

Courtesy of Gloria Stevens Figure Salons.

Figure 1–1. In this release, important information is at the beginning.
Notice that a contact person is mentioned as well as when
the release can be used.

reader does not stop to wonder why a sentence is included. Read the next
example of a *confusing* story:

Oil spills in coastal waters are increasing at an alarming rate and
federal authorities lack the technology to control these spills, a
Congressman warned today.

Rep. Harrison L. Smith told a House Subcommittee in Boston that the
Argo Merchant oil spill cannot be viewed as an isolated incident.

Oil spills are common now, Congressman Smith stated, and the federal government does not have the knowledge or equipment to solve the problem.

Congressman Smith is well known for his interest in ecology, and in his district he has sponsored several educational programs on the subject.

It's the last paragraph that's confusing the issue. A better story would deal only with the Congressman's testimony at the subcommittee hearing, not with his sponsorship of ecology programs.

Transitionals. Sometimes certain words (*transitionals*) can be used to tie paragraphs together. The next story covers a banker's convention where there were two speakers on the same program. One speaker is the lead and the practitioner works in the second speaker (third paragraph) by using a transitional:

The State Banking Commissioner warned bankers today they will have to extend banking hours in the evening and on Saturday before the approval of any new branches.

Commissioner Frances B. Byrnes spoke at the Savings Banker's Convention in Newington. He said, "If a bank fails to have evening and Saturday hours, we will not approve a new branch for that bank."

Another speaker at the convention, Martin L. Lynch, bank financial consultant, forecast an excellent year for mortgages.

"New housing starts have increased by 22%, which means more mortgages will be granted by the thrift institutions," Mr. Lynch said.

Or the practitioner could write:

A second speaker, Martin L. Lynch, bank financial consultant, forecast . . .

By using these word cues (*another speaker, a second speaker*) the reader is aware that the bank commissioner section is concluded and another speaker is now the subject. Another example of transition:

John P. Jones was re-elected president of the Union Club at the annual meeting last night at the Fairmount Restaurant.

Mr. Jones is serving his fifth term as club president, the oldest men's social club in the city. Mr. Jones is a local attorney.

In other business, members voted to hold the club's annual Christmas party for disadvantaged children on December 23 at the YMCA.

"In other business" is a simple transition, allowing the writer to combine two stories.

Two-topic leads

Sometimes when a news release is written dealing with two separate topics or actions, the practitioner combines both topics in the lead—or if not in the lead, in the second or third paragraph. The reader is thus told in the lead to anticipate another topic later in the story.

> Construction of a new corporate headquarters in Watertown and the purchase of the privately owned XYG Company were announced today by the AAA Corporation.
>
> John G. Fuller, president of the AAA Corporation, said in the joint announcement that the construction of the 30-story, all-glass building will start in May. It is expected to be completed in three years.
>
> The new building, which will be located on a 20-acre site on Broadway, Madison, and Freemont streets, will cost $50,000,000, Mr. Fuller estimated.
>
> The AAA Corporation's present headquarters will be used as the corporation's computer center when the new building is completed.
>
> In the second announcement, Mr. Fuller said the newly acquired XYG Company will operate as a separate entity. He emphasized there are no present plans to change or remove any personnel.
>
> "The XYG Corporation is privately owned and it was felt by the owners that it should be connected with a large corporation," Mr. Fuller said.
>
> "The larger corporation could aid the company in its plan to expand internationally, especially in markets where the AAA Corporation now is doing business."
>
> No purchase price for the XYG Company was announced. The 75-year-old company manufactures specialized dressings for surgical use.

The summary lead with both of the story's announcements (construction of the new headquarters and the company purchase) tells the reader to expect that the topic will change.

Identification

Usually news releases inform about an organization, individual, group, government agency, or company. In most releases at least one person is mentioned if not several. Each person mentioned is identified so that the reader knows who the person is and why he or she is in the story.

For example, George P. Donaldson is president of the XYG Corporation. While all his employees know who he is, the general public does not. A confusing news release about the company being awarded a contract reads:

> The XYG Corporation has been awarded a government contract for the construction of 16 radar installations along the Eastern seaboard, it was announced today.
> George P. Donaldson said the Navy had notified the company that they were the lowest bidders.

The question is, *Who is George P. Donaldson?* Is he a Navy spokesperson or with the XYG Company? He might even be a person who heard about the contract and told a reporter.

Key identification devices. Three devices aid in identifying people in the news release: title, phrase in apposition, and prepositional phrase.

First, those people with a public title (governor, mayor, judge, commissioner) are identified with the title capitalized before their name.

> Four streets were closed today by Street Commissioner John P. Huntington.

> Chief Justice Mary G. Gillen of the Municipal Court cautioned fellow judges today that most traffic violators are repeaters.

> Mayor Charles A. Ross signed three orders today for the construction of a number of ballparks within the city.

Sometimes people can be identified with a title even though the title is not official.

> A warning that certain plastic toys may be unsafe for preschool children was issued today by consumer advocate James P. Herter at a news conference.

In this example, Mr. Herter does not hold a public office, but he has earned an unofficial title through past publicity.

Second, a writer can use the phrase in apposition. Set off by two commas at the beginning and end, it identifies the position or status of a person without an official title.

> Roger P. Billings, research director of the Dane Drug Company, said the new drug, titled *DMY,* has been tested thoroughly and is safe.

Notice when a person has a status important to the story:

> Marion L. Johnson, third grade teacher at the Cochituate School, told the School Committee she needed more room because of her student load.

Third, the writer can use the prepositional phrase, which does not use commas. It often identifies the organizational background of the individual.

> Dr. Martin J. Leonard of the East Medical Center warned today that elderly men and women should not attempt to exercise or walk in extreme temperatures.

> Julian G. George of the Planned Parenthood League asked that birth-control literature be distributed by the churches to married couples.

Sentence structure

Sometimes even an experienced writer finds it difficult to write a simple sentence. In explaining an action or technicality, the writer may become too involved and write sentences that are difficult to understand. In your releases, prefer the simple sentence to the complex. If possible, place the subject at the beginning of the sentence:

> Members of the organization successfully fought their way through the legal restrictions.

This sentence is simple and the subject (*members of the organization*) is at the beginning. The sentence could have been written:

> There were a number of legal restrictions that the organization faced, but the members hired attorneys, fought each restriction and ultimately won out.

This compound sentence does not clearly say that the organization won over the restrictions.

Verbs: Passive and active

Writers need action words to make stories come alive. Thus it is important to know that verbs may be active or passive, depending on whether the subject performs the action (active) or receives the action (passive). Whereas the active voice is a single verb (The president *awarded* three scholarships), the passive voice is a verb phrase (Three scholarships *were awarded* by the president). Notice that in the passive, the auxiliary of the phrase is a form of *to be* followed by the past participle.

Because of its force and immediacy, most writers prefer the active voice. It gives the reader a sense of action. On the other hand, use the passive voice when your subject is unimportant, unknown, or obvious. Passives weaken the emphasis of an important noun or pronoun and make the sentence wordy, as in this confusing example:

> A proposal by the union to insure all family members of employees of the company for dental care was approved today by the company president.

In this story, the idea that the proposal was approved is tucked away at the end of the sentence because of the use of the passive voice. It should read:

> The company president today approved dental care insurance for all family members of employees.

In addition, remember that it's awkward and confusing if the voice is changed during a sentence. For example, this sentence starts in the active voice and then shifts to the passive:

> Committee member Jones voted approval to widen the street, and approval was also voted for by committee member Higgins.

> Better:

> Committee members Jones and Higgins voted for approval to widen the street.

Feature stories

Feature stories differ from news stories. Simply, a news story has a time element; it must be used immediately if it is to be relevant. (For example: *The election of officers will be held Tuesday.*) But a feature story does not have this immediacy; it may be used today, tomorrow, next week, or next month and still be valid.

Other differences include style and content. In features, the writing is more relaxed than in news stories; the lead paragraph does not have to contain the five *W*'s and an *H*. This is because whereas a news story is written for its news value, a feature story informs, entertains or even educates the reader about an idea. Sentences can be longer than twenty words (the average news sentence length). Here's an example of a feature:

The archives of the Sullivan Company are full of fascinating lore family business that stretches back before the Civil War.

In fact, the founder, John H. Sullivan, started the business by selling seeds to New Hampshire farmers when he tired of farming those rocky hills.

Mr. Sullivan sold seed on credit and collected payments when the vegetables were harvested. He fought with the Union Troops during the Civil War, was wounded at Bull Run and returned to New Hampshire without a leg.

Within five years, Mr. Sullivan was a millionaire, supplying farm goods not only to New England farmers but to those on their way to open the West.

Mr. Sullivan's seven sons were his sales force. Ever since that time, only direct descendants of the founder have headed the business.

The company's taciturnity stems from the fact that it is one of a diminishing breed of enterprises, the family-founded, family-owned New England company. It clings to the old business tradition of disclosing as little as possible; it recoils from the thought of "going public."

In this story, the feature writer takes a liberty with the lead, arousing curiosity with a statement not fully explained. Not until the sixth paragraph is the story's focus fully clear: "the family-founded New England company."

Although most feature writers develop a style, the average practitioner may write the story "straight," and it will be quite acceptable.

For the writer in public relations, most companies, institutions, or organizations have many opportunities for good features. Such features center around a personality, such as an officer with a unique hobby or an employee who is an amateur inventor. Other features relate the company or organization to the public's needs. For example, an oil company could do a story on ways to save fuel during the winter months; a bank could explain interest rates on various loans; a religious group could explain changes in its services. As you can see, then, a professional writer discovers material for features by using his imagination.

Here's an example of an oil company feature:

There are seven ways to economize on oil consumption this winter.

The Atha Oil Company, in a bulletin, tells its customers not to open windows or doors for any length of time. It also recommends that home owners invest in storm windows, even temporary ones.

Insulation on outside walls is a must and the temperature of the house should never be above 68 degrees.

Before retiring, residents should lower the temperature to 60 degrees. The oil burner should be checked by a competent serviceperson to make sure it's efficient.

Any openings, however small, should be blocked off, so no cold air seeps through.

"With this energy crisis, we must strive to save fuel," John G. Gordon, company president, said. "It is common sense and if everyone cooperates, we can save 25% of our fuel this year."

In this feature the lead is straight: there are seven ways to economize on oil consumption, and these ways are explained.

Another example:

Interest rates are so varied at banks these days that many potential savers are confused.

Interest rates vary for different savings accounts, Frankland F. Milton, vice-president of the City Savings Bank, explained.

A regular savings account (one in which the depositor may withdraw funds at any time) pays less interest, seven percent annually, than an account in which the depositor must notify the bank 90 days in advance of withdrawal. That type of account pays nine percent annually.

NOW accounts, those savings accounts that allow check writing privileges without service charges, pay five percent annually, Mr. Milton said.

He added the reason a depositor is paid nine percent for the 90-day account is that the bank has a longer time to invest the deposit money than it does for a regular savings account. Therefore, the bank pays more interest for this type of account.

The regular savings account pays more interest than the NOW account, because the bank does not have to grant check writing privileges with a regular account, Mr. Milton explained.

The lead in this feature is simple and right to the point: Interest rates are so varied that savers are confused. After this statement of fact, the reader will continue the story and to find out why. The story explains, in simple terms, how the rate structure works.

Finally, story unity is as important in a feature as it is in a news story. There must be a reason for each sentence to be included; it must enhance the story. For example, in the previous story on banking the writer could have said:

Most banks have safe deposit boxes.

But obviously this sentence does not belong and would throw the story's continuity off. So, even though features are more relaxed than news stories, they still must be written tightly and to the point.

Summary

To the working public relations practitioner, the news release is a vital tool—an economical and efficient way to reach the general public. Because the practitioner is a professional communicator, he knows that the news media is a good way to inform the mass public. As such, he must be skilled in writing releases.

The news release and its use in the media

An editor reads hundreds of stories a day by the news staff, wire services, and public relations people. How does an editor decide which to use? He must judge each story on a set of criteria called *news judgment* or *value*, and it's important for the public relations practitioner to understand what these criteria are. This chapter will cover the seven basic values and details behind how news releases are used in the media of print and broadcast.

News judgment criteria

Proximity

A news release about an event, institution, company, organization, or individual within the circulation range of a newspaper or broadcast area of a radio station is considered local. Such stories would interest the area residents. To the school, college, or armed forces practitioner, sending a release to a local paper is known as "home towning" a release. For example, he may write a release about Mary Jones being a member of the freshman class of CVY College. It is sent to Mary's hometown newspaper and is used by the editor because the residents are interested in Mary Jones. If the practitioner wrote about the college without Mary's name in the story, the editor would discard it because the college is outside his paper's circulation area.

Prominence

The importance of the story's focus, be it a company or even a public issue, plays a critical role in the judgment of a story. Obviously a relatively unknown company's news release has less chance of being mentioned in the paper than one from General Motors. Likewise, a hotly debated public issue has little difficulty breaking into the media. Remember that what's considered controversial changes from year to year.

Timeliness

Time is the essence of news. An editor would discard a story on the election of officers of an organization turned in a month or two after the election.

Impact

How an event affects the lives of the readers or listeners in an area is important to an editor. For example, a jump in the inflation rate affects everyone, so such a story has impact. Sometimes companies close, drastically changing the lives of many residents. Such stories always have impact.

Magnitude

Magnitude refers to an event or occurrence involving a large number of people. (Unlike impact, the idea of magnitude does *not* involve great damage or good fortune.) For example, an estimated 1,000,000 men, women, and children attended a concert and firework display on the Charles River Esplanade in Boston in celebration of the nation's 200th birthday. If only several hundred people attended, the story would not have received the tremendous coverage it did.

In addition, magnitude is relative, depending on the circulation of the newspaper or the audience of the radio station. If 5,000 people had attended a similar concert and display in a small town, that story number would still have had magnitude for the local news editor.

Conflict

Conflict refers to verbal or physical clashes or confrontations. The public relations practitioner is usually on one side of a conflict. For example, he may represent a company against which a union is striking, or a protest group demanding a change in its organization's rules.

Oddity

In simplistic terms, oddity is "man bites dog." Because such stories are always interesting to readers, many editors look for a twist in a story (or, as it is known in radio, the "kicker"). The twist is always something out of the ordinary, the opposite of what is expected.

Working with the media

Deadlines

The public relations practitioner must understand deadlines for print and broadcast. An excellent rule to practice is to get the news release on the news desk at least twenty-four hours before the story is scheduled for use. With this lead time, an editor or a reporter has time to "work on" the story. The story might be completely rewritten or the editor might wish additional information. Some practitioners argue that the deadline for news pages of a mass circulation daily (a paper with more than 100,000 circulation) is three to four hours before edition time, but this deadline is really only for the paper's own staff. Most editors would not consider a release reaching the news desk at deadline; he's too busy with the news from the staff and wire services to pay attention to such a release.

Remember that the sectional pages of the mass circulation dailies have earlier deadlines than the news pages. Most dailies are morning papers, with news pages deadline for the first edition at seven o'clock; however, the women's section deadline would be three hours earlier.

The middle-sized dailies (circulation from 50,000 to 100,000) and the small dailies (under 50,000 circulation) publish in the afternoon with a usual midmorning (10:00 A.M.) deadline. In contrast, weekly newspapers publish on Wednesday or Thursday and have varying deadlines, some Monday at noon, others Tuesday at noon. Some even have Friday deadlines.

A few public relations practitioners of varied competence claim their friendship with editors and reporters enable them to receive special consideration for their clients' news releases. It is true that certain practitioners have the respect of those in the news media and their releases are given full consideration. But these practitioners earn respect through professionalism and competence; practitioners trading on their acquaintance with a reporter to get a release used seldom succeed regularly. The latter soon wear out their welcome.

The competent professional practitioner is an asset to the media. His knowledge of a company or institution can be an aid to a working reporter, who relies on accurate and honest information.

Some practitioners mail news releases to a number of reporters and editors employed by the same newspaper, radio, or television station, hoping that one might use the story. This practice leads to confusion and mistrust among the media people. If the editor of the metropolitan section decides to use the release and a writer for the women's pages incorporates it into a column, the managing editor would be furious.

Who covers what

It's not difficult to discover who covers the different news beats or story categories, even in the largest newspapers or broadcast news departments. You can use one of a number of directories listing reporters and writers and their specialities or call the paper or station. If your release must be used on a certain day and you're not sure the writer is working that day, send it to the writer's department.

Most practitioners compile a mailing list with the names of the writers and broadcasters. However, because of frequent personnel changes, it is difficult to keep the list current. If you have doubts about who the writer is, address the release to the person's job title: *Medical*

Editor, Financial Editor, Labor Editor, Consumer Editor, School Editor, etc., depending on the release subject. A general release would be sent to the *City Desk, News Editor,* or simply *Editor.*

Submitting the release

As mentioned previously, a tightly written release, short and to the point, fares better than a long story, so write accordingly.

When submitting the release, you might use company release paper with the company's name, address, and telephone number printed on the paper. Some companies print their name in bright colors to attract the editor's attention. Seldom, however, will vivid colors convince an editor that a news release has value.

The printed or typed name of the company or organization, with the name of the person to contact, is placed on the top left-hand corner of the page. Information about the person to contact includes business and home telephone numbers because reporters work around the clock, weekends, and holidays, and they may want more details. For example:

WERS CORPORATION
333 MAIN ST.
BOSTON, MA 02116
Contact: John J. Jones, 295 5678 days
                           367 2345 evenings, weekends

Below the name and address, triple space and type in the release date:

Immediate Release
Release, Dec. 15, A.M.
Release, June 12, 3 P.M.

Immediate release means the story can be used as soon as the media receives it. The date and A.M. release means the story can be used any time that morning and thereafter. The date and specific P.M. release means the story can be used at 3 P.M. and thereafter. Use the specific time release when an announcement is being made at that time, or a speech is being delivered, etc.

Most newspeople honor release dates within reason. The practitioner's responsibility is to have the release delivered at approximately the same time to each news desk.

News releases for broadcast

Many practitioners send the same release to radio and television news departments as they do to newspapers. They argue that their releases work and that they do not have to write separately for print and broadcast. However, good broadcasts are written for the ear. A release specially prepared for broadcast helps the broadcast writer, and the story has an edge over the release written for print. In contrast to a reporter, a newscaster writes in conversational style with relatively short sentences.

In broadcast news releases, identify the subject of the release by job title before the name of the subject:

> The president of the National Harbor Trust Company, Horace H. Hilton, warned today . . .

This technique identifies the subject of the story for the listener, who may not be paying close attention to a radio or even a television newscast. Whereas an interested newspaper reader can reread a sentence if there is a misunderstanding, the broadcast listener does not have this luxury because a sentence is never repeated on the same broadcast. Thus, sentences in broadcast writing must be written to the point of oversimplification.

Although newscasts written conversationally permit incomplete sentences, most seasoned practitioners write short but complete sentences. The incomplete sentence technique requires skill and practice without the practitioner becoming verbose. The discipline in writing a short but complete sentence solves the problem.

Release length many times determines whether a story is to be used on a newscast. The story should be on one page, two or three paragraphs at the most, even if the same release for newspapers runs two pages. The average news story runs thirty seconds or less in a newscast, approximately sixty-five words (three sentences of twenty words each). If *who, what, when, where, why,* and *how* are included in the sixty-five words, the story stands on its own. Many writers read the broadcast release out loud, allowing themselves to hear the copy and catch any errors.

You can supply the same release to radio and television. The television editor might feel the story warrants a visual presentation and sends a film crew or, at times, you will want to supply a film clip or slide to go with the release.

News releases for the trade press

The trade press plays an important role in the communications of a business or industry. The trade press consists of those magazines and newspapers devoting their editorial and advertising space to one business or industry. Each business, trade, industry, and profession has its own press. Some of the publications, as in the electronics industry, are as sophisticated in design and writing style as any "slick" magazines on the newstands. Other publications leave much to be desired not only in editorial content but in design and makeup.

It's difficult to categorize these newspapers and magazines because there are thousands of them and each one is different. Many are understaffed and their editors welcome legitimate news releases.

Most of the trade publications have thirty days before publication deadline. The rule of getting a news release into the publication in ample time holds for the trade press as it does the regular press.

Before writing a release, study the publication to discover its editorial depth and format—then write the release to fit that format. As in a news story, use the five *W's* and an *H* when writing.

Many of the publications are feature oriented, and a well-written feature usually is acceptable. Most of the magazines look for profiles on the company itself or the chief executive officers. First you should suggest the story to the editor, giving the vital statistics. You then wait until the editor approves the story and allows you to write it.

Always write objectively and accurately. You may submit a layout of photographs. Usually, both editor and client are pleased with the story.

Most industrial publications run a "new products" column in which they print a paragraph and, at times, a photo of a new product or the redesign of an existing product. Mention in the new product column usually means additional business to the manufacturer. The paragraph must be concise and accurate. Because the information for the paragraph may be taken from an engineer's manual, you may need to make the terminology more understandable. Thus you must comprehend the product and its significance before writing.

Photos and captions

Photos for newspapers should be black and white, glossy finish, crisp and clear. The printing process demands photographs of professional quality—not too light or too dark, in good focus. Do not send a photograph if its quality is questionable; your professional reputation would not be enhanced.

Captions identify photographs sent to newspapers and other publications. Captions are miniature stories; each stands on its own and does not need an accompanying story to explain what it is about.

Many newspapers have photo editors, who make all picture decisions. Thus your news release may go to one editor and your photo to another. For this reason, identify all photos. Each person or subject— even in a group photo—is identified by name and title in the caption, with an explanation why he, she, or it appears in the photograph. The caption, typewritten and double-spaced on a sheet of release paper, carries the same release date as the news release accompanying the photo or photos. Caption each photo, even if a single photo is sent with the release and the person in the photo obviously is the subject of the story. Here's an example of a good caption:

> FOUR ELECTED TO BOARD—Four prominent citizens, left to right, Judge Harold G. Hodgkinson, Dr. Myron G. Collins, Francis D. Higgins, president of Higgins Co., and John H. Wheatley, vice-president of the Milton Bank, were elected members of the Board of Trustees at the annual meeting of Milton Hospital.

In this caption, the writer names the four members and tells why the photo was published. Whether a story on the annual meeting appears in the newspaper or not, the caption stands on its own.

You can attach captions several ways: scotch-taped to the back of the photo and then folded over so the copy is in front; pasted on the back of the photo; pasted on the photo's margin and attached with a paper clip to the photo. Some people even print the caption on the back of the photo with a lithographic pencil. Editors prefer the caption typewritten and scotch-taped to the photograph. Paper clips can tear or dent a photo; paste on the front can damage the picture; pen or pencil (not lithographic) on the back of the photo dents the front; felt-tip pen bleeds and permeates the photo's glossy front.

Summary

Editors choose releases based on these criteria: proximity, prominence, timeliness, impact, magnitude, conflict, and oddity. In working with the media, you must understand their deadlines and submit releases to them in a clear fashion. Releases for broadcasts should be done in a simple, conversational style. The trade press often desires features and factual articles on products. When submitting photos, identify all persons by using a caption. Never use paperclips, pencils, pens, or paste on photos. Always submit photos of good quality.

Brochures, pamphlets, and booklets

Frequently practitioners write and produce brochures, pamphlets, and booklets to inform or educate the public about a problem that is for the most part unknown or unnoticed.

Such is the case of the chronic disease foundations (heart, arthritis, cancer, kidney) who fight for recognition and financial support from the public. These associations must advertise the problem and ask for financial support for research for the eventual control or cure of the disease. The association's practitioner uses both print and broadcast to win recognition from the public. However, because of space and time limitations in the mass media, the full impact of the message sometimes is lost. A second step in his campaign is to send material to those interested or potentially interested in helping with a donation or some type of support.

Multiple sclerosis is a case in point. This disease was virtually unknown until a high-powered educational campaign was launched through the mass media. The campaign included the distribution of pamphlets and brochures that explained the problem in layman's language.

Production and layout

If the public relations goal is to persuade a certain group to change an attitude or opinion, the only effective method to reach the members of this group might be to mail a brochure to reach each residence. Although such information is not *sales* promotional, the brochures are similar to ads in appearance. Physical size of the piece and the space for the message (the copy blocks) directs the length of the copy to be written. Take a piece of paper the size of the brochure or pamphlet and fold it the way the finished piece will be (a *dummy*). This technique gives you a visual indication of how much copy you must write. (See Figure 3–1.)

Will there be illustrations, photographs, line drawings, or charts? Where will these illustrations be? Will the front of the piece have a title or headline? Decide all this before writing the copy.

The method of distribution also governs the size of the piece. If it is to be mailed, will an envelope be used, or will the address be typed on the outside cover? Space must be left for the address and stamp if no envelope is used. What size envelope will be used? Will the material fit a standard size, such as a number 10 envelope (regular-size business envelope), or will special envelopes be needed? Pamphlets distributed to the public usually are placed in literature racks. Make sure the pamphlet or booklet fits in the rack compartments. Finally, check with the printer to make sure the piece can be printed on standard-sized paper without problems. Remember that brochures and pamphlets are folded, not bound. Booklets are bound with pages in multiples of four: four, eight, twelve, sixteen, twenty, twenty-four, etc.

The common printing method for such materials is offset. From the dummy you will know the approximate number of words, sentences, and paragraphs to write to fit in the copy block or blocks. An artist or typesetter "specs" the type, meaning that he determines the size and style of the type to be used in the piece and relates this information on the copy to the composing room. (See p. 42.) A composition house then sets type

Figure 3–1. An artist's layout for a brochure or pamphlet, indicating headlines, photos, and type.

and returns the copy in galley form for you (the writer) to proof. Correct the proofs (those typographical errors made by you or the typesetter in the original copy) and return the galleys for correction.

An artist then pastes up the corrected type on an illustration board, each panel or page of the piece as it will be printed. The makeup of the panel or page allows space for the illustration. You will check the boards and release them to the printer. The printer shows you a final proof and paper samples before going to press.

It's important that you're sure of the copy before setting it in type. Copy changes, other than typographical corrections, add to the printing bill. The typesetter calls each changed line *author's alterations* and charges accordingly.

Courtesy of the Arthritis Foundation.

Figure 3–2. Brochures showing various cover designs and back-cover logos.

Writing styles

Write the brochure using the public relations purpose as a guide. The readers' knowledge of the subject will further guide you, especially if the brochure or pamphlet is educational or informational. Readers' attitudes and opinions on controversial subjects are also very important. Will the majority of those reading the piece be friendly, hostile, or indifferent to your side of the issue?

Argumentation

Argumentation style tries to persuade the reader about the merits of a specific side of an issue. The writer must have a sense of audience to successfully write in this style. He anticipates the thoughts and feelings of his audience and then expresses these thoughts and feelings in words familiar to the members of that group. The inexperienced practitioner may feel this impossible. How can you know the feelings and thoughts of others? Remember such brochures are directed to a specific audience known to the company or organization. The sensitive practitioner anticipates the readers' reaction and objections with little difficulty. He then tries to resolve these objections in the copy.

In argumentation, there are several ways to start the copy. You can state a fact or premise, propose a question, or introduce a sentence or two giving both sides of the problem situation.

For example, one practitioner's goal was to persuade a group of opinion leaders throughout the country to speak to members of Congress to revamp the student loan program.

He realized that an emotional appeal would fall on deaf ears because his audience consisted of professional men and women, mass communicators, and business and industrial executives. These men and women would base their decision only on fact. His style would have to be logical, slightly formal. The copy read:

> The guaranteed student loan program for undergraduates needs revamping.
>
> Presidents of five major universities, Harvard, Yale, Princeton, Cornell, and Williams, have called the need urgent. The presidents have written Congressional leaders asking for immediate legislation to change this program.
>
> In the joint letter, the presidents said: "Undergraduate loan programs are failing, as is clear from the cumulative $385 million default total. When we encourage full-need students (those with little or no family

support) to contract debts totalling seven thousand or more, we encourage a practice that would be financially ill-advised for even middle-income families."

The burden is particularly severe on undergraduates enrolled in independent schools or colleges. Already there exists a considerable tuition gap between students enrolled in taxpayer-supported colleges and universities and those who choose the independent sector.

This gap should not be narrowed by raising tuition at taypayer-supported institutions. There should be a tuition equalization program, a program that would make additional grants available, on the basis of need, to undergraduates in the independent sector.

Through existing loan programs, Congress has already inadvertently pointed the way towards a new coming of age. It will be the rite of passage separating not boys and girls from men and women, but separating the adolescent student from the true adult.

In this rite, young Americans will declare bankruptcy at about 25 and thus be freed of all debts incurred in obtaining their education. This new rite of passage will undermine the concept of financial responsibility, which is very closely related to personal integrity.

Some form of it may become morally acceptable if we continue the present emphasis on loans as the basic form of educational assistance.

To be sure, not all Americans will opt for bankruptcy, but those who are so old fashioned as to shun it may opt for a life of debt.

Congress also must deal with the problem of equity when families in the private or independent sector pay the same taxes as families of students in the state-subsidized sector.

If the independent or private sector did not exist, the cost of the education would have to be borne by the state.

These families actually save the taxpayers of America the cost of educating 2.2 million students each year. The value of these savings to the taxpayer is tremendous, though it is a back-breaking burden for the families of many of these students.

It will be far less expensive to the taxpayer if he lightens this burden and thereby preserves the independent sector and equality of choice.

The taxpayer should compare the cost of operating the independent or private sector with the cost of saving it. It could be saved by a tuition equalization program that would award grants to students in the independent sector ranging from $200 to $1,500, based on a need formula that would make the average award $1,000.

Please contact your senator and congressman and tell him how you feel about the program. As the presidents wrote, it is urgent.

This brochure copy has a sense of audience, the choice of words and combination of words focussed on the successful, well-informed man and woman, a leader, educated, slightly conservative. The opening sentence is right to the point: The guaranteed student loan program for undergraduates needs revamping. The rest of the copy reinforces this statement. Notice that argumentation requires the use of details and facts. The writer's sense of audience dictates how many and what kinds of facts he uses. In this narrative, the writer mentions the default total and the idea that many young people may declare bankruptcy or face a debt-ridden life. Finally, he presents a solution to the problem with a request that the reader take action. He assumes correctly that his audience will be sympathetic.

Another example:

Proponents of the use of laetrille proclaim it is an effective treatment against certain types of cancer. The U. S. Food and Drug Administration outlaws laetrille from interstate shipment, stating there is no tangible evidence that the drug affects cancer either in test animals or humans.

Proponents of the drug claim they have documentary proof that patients do improve, at least for a while, after laetrille therapy.

They further argue physical improvement and pain relief result from the compound's psychological effects even if laetrille does not cure certain cancers.

Many physicians practice this type of psychological treatment. Advocates point to the use of placebo, which the medical profession has used since early in the 19th century to describe inactive substances or procedures used with a patient under the guise of physically effective treatment.

The theory (the patient really believes in it, so it works) has been used by physicians in many cultures and civilizations. From the dark ages until now, an era of supposed medical enlightenment, the placebo has been a potent and versatile tool for the relief of suffering. Today faith healing has taken its place in our world.

If all this is true, and even if laetrille does not have a tangible effect for cancer cure, could we not allow it? Is the Food and Drug Administration so rigid it can't bend just one time? Those cancer victims who believe in the drug then could easily get laetrille, and on humane grounds alone, this would be a blessing.

If the Food and Drug Administration did bend "just this once" and permitted interstate shipment, would it really do any harm?

Or could it, in fact, set a precedent? Could it not open the door for other drugs, some even harmful to a person, that the Administration has banned? Could not the manufacturers of banned drugs argue they should be allowed on the market for psychological reasons?

When the Food and Drug Administration allows a drug to be shipped interstate, it gives that drug a legitimacy, a sense that the administration approves the drug.

Since early in the 19th century, legitimate drug manufacturers and the government have fought to regulate and control the manufacture of drugs. It's been a long, hard struggle.

The Food and Drug Administration was founded, in part, to wage this fight, the control of drugs. We cannot allow a backward step despite a strong emotional appeal.

Drugs must be tested for effectiveness under controlled, scientific conditions. Government approval must be based on the findings of these tests.

To approve the effectiveness of laetrille without legitimate, scientific evidence is, indeed, a step backwards.

In this case, the writer wanted to speak directly to the opinion leaders charged with decision whether or not to override the federal government and allow physicians in their states to prescribe laetrille. He knew before writing that for the most part, the men and women of his audience were undecided. Thus he felt the best approach would be to present both sides of the question fairly, even noting that there may be psychological value in the drug. He ends the brochure with a strong, unemotional conclusion.

Success in argumentation is achieved when two basic factors are met by the writer. The first is clearness; the reader must understand what the message is about. The second is forcefulness; the strength of the argument convinces the reader to the writer's point of view. Structurally, these factors are achieved by an accurate choice of words and tight, concise sentences. Simply, the reader must be able to read the copy easily. If there are too many words or vague terms, the reader slows down, becomes frustrated and loses interest.

Specifically, nouns and verbs move a sentence and bring force to the message, especially in argumentation. Use of an adjective means less than a noun is being used and use of an adverb means less than a verb is being used.

Keep in mind that a reader naturally assumes he will understand the message. If he's confused at the end of the copy, inner conflict occurs, not persuasion.

Descriptive

Descriptive writing persuades the reader, not by detail and fact as in argumentation, but by exercising the imagination. In this style, the writer uses the reader's imagination to recreate an experience, either real or imagined. He gives the reader the illusion of participation.

In this example of descriptive writing, the author is speaking to college-age men, 19 to 21. He asks them to volunteer as Big Brothers.

At 10, it can be very lonely and frightening. Remember how confused you were when you were 10 years old?

There were times when you wished you wouldn't get any older. The world seemed so big and you were confused.

But there was someone who really understood what it was like. He helped you see the road clearly ahead. It wasn't so confusing then.

Your dad was the one. He shared his experience and wisdom with you; it really helped a lot.

What if your dad wasn't there to help and share? If there was no one really to understand what it was like to be 10, someone older, a man.

If there was no one to guide you over those rough, growing-up spots, no one older to show the way.

That's what Big Brother is all about, showing the way.

The copy is short and asks the college man to remember back to the age of ten. The reader uses his imagination to remember those uncertain days of being just ten.

You're old, without a car, and you live alone in a neighborhood with no public transportation. You have to walk every place you go.

There is no bus to the nearest large community. The bus stop is three miles away.

If you run out of butter or some other staple, the nearest store is a mile and a half away. You shop at the town's only supermarket once a week. A neighbor gives you a lift, but there is no set pattern. She may go on Monday or Wednesday or Friday. You have to be ready when she is.

Other shopping needs are accomplished the same way. You are invited as a guest.

A doctor's appointment can be a crisis. It is difficult to find someone to give you a lift. And on your fixed income, you can't afford a taxi.

There are no close relatives. You are old, retired, and without anyone you can rely on.

This is not an isolated case. There are a number of men and women in our community facing similar problems.

We ask that you volunteer a half a day a month, driving Golden Age citizens to and from a store or to the doctor.

If we have enough volunteers, we can have this daily service for our older neighbors and friends.

Only a half day per month.

This brochure could be mailed through a community asking for volunteers, especially homemakers. In it, the writer tries to present a word picture, easily imagined by the reader. Obviously, word selection plays an important role in this style.

Narrative

Narrative writing differs from argumentation and descriptive in that it is for the most part organized chronologically rather than by logic of thought or development of feeling. Chronological organization allows a wide range; the writer can follow a number of avenues. Narratives include illustration, example, and description. Sometimes it may seem that the chronology of events is superficial, but it is a good unification system. For example:

> In August 1959, Dr. William Augustus Hinton passed away in his 76th year. He left behind him a lifetime of distinguished service to mankind, medical science, and education.
>
> A brilliant man of varied talents, Dr. Hinton was the first black man to be granted a full professorship at Harvard Medical School. He founded the Hinton Course Laboratory Technicians at the Boston Dispensary, and he originated the universally accepted Hinton test for syphilis.
>
> Dr. Hinton's rise to fame in the medical world is like a Horatio Alger story. The son of former slaves, Dr. Hinton was born in Chicago and raised in Kansas. He graduated the youngest in his high school's history and completed three years of premedical work in two at the University of Kansas. The financial problems he faced while at school would have defeated a lesser man.
>
> Dr. Hinton finished his undergraduate work at Harvard College on a scholarship. He began teaching at various colleges in Tennessee and Oklahoma and married Ada Hawes, a teacher.
>
> In 1909, Dr. Hinton and his wife returned to Boston. He entered Harvard Medical School and although seven years had passed since his premedical studies, he completed his medical education in three years instead of four.
>
> Upon graduation, Dr. Hinton worked at Harvard's Wasserman Laboratory, where he studied the serology of syphilis. In 1915, he was placed in charge of the laboratory.
>
> A vivid lecturer at Harvard, Simmons, and Tufts, Dr. Hinton was hailed in the *New England Journal of Medicine* as having had "a flair for rolling rhetoric that often left students applauding in the aisles."
>
> Dr. Hinton was then named pathologist-in-chief of the Boston Dispensary, and he remained associated with that institution until his retirement in 1952.
>
> During the period from 1927 to 1935, Dr. Hinton was publishing the results of his research. His research lead to the development of the Hinton test and the completion of his book, *Syphilis and its Treatment.*

In 1929 Dr. Hinton saw the need for well-trained personnel to perform routine laboratory tests. He developed a program at the Boston Dispensary to train young high school graduates as laboratory technicians.

In addition, college-trained technicians would have the responsibility for special techniques, supervision, and research.

Dr. Hinton fought to build the program's reputation, which prompted the Harvard Medical School Alumni Magazine to comment: "The school gained such an excellent reputation that many professional schools began to offer similar courses."

Shortly after Dr. Hinton's death, a committee was formed to recommend a fitting memorial to perpetuate the memory of this man's work.

Dr. Hinton's dedication to the training program motivated the committee to decide that his work should continue.

They decided that an endowment be obtained to provide the directorship of the school, bearing Dr. Hinton's name. It will be a living memorial to one of America's great medical educators and scientists.

The brochure on Dr. Hinton includes illustration and description, and basically it is organized chronologically, following the major steps of Dr. Hinton's professional career.

Note that because the writer was addressing a sympathetic audience, there was no need for argumentation to plead Dr. Hinton's contribution to medical education and science.

Summary

Copy for brochures and pamphlets must be concise. Space for the message is usually "tight"; you do not have the luxury of writing reams of copy. As a general rule, the message when set in type reduces one third from the typewritten copy. If there are ten typewritten words to a line and there are thirty lines, the type would be set in twenty lines of ten words each. This varies with the type size, but it is a good general guide.

No matter what style you choose, keep the sentences short, the words accurate in their definition. The goal is communication; the reader must understand what the message is about. You cannot persuade if the reader can't comprehend what you've said.

You must decide what style of writing best tells the message effectively. *Persuasion* calls for either argumentation or description (depending on the audience, their attitude, and the message content). *Narration,* organized chronologically, usually is effective in an educational or informational brochure.

The style of writing and method of distribution dictates the organization of the copy, and the message points to whether illustrations should be used or not and of what type. Naturally the illustrations are placed to coincide with the text's message.

Most brochures, pamphlets, and booklets are printed offset. A composition house sets the type and you will proof for typographical errors and for pasteup.

The annual report

Publicly held companies (those companies selling shares of stock to the general public either through stock exchanges or "over the counter") are required to report annually to their shareholders. The report describes the company's performance during the year by narrative, graphics, and financial statements. Many companies supply their reports to the financial community, business writers and editors, security analysts, stockbrokers, and potential investors, especially mutual fund buyers.

Some companies print their financial information in a separate supplement and send both the annual report and supplement to stockholders and members of the financial community. They send the annual report alone to customers and other interested companies and individuals in the industry.

The financial information in the annual report is standardized by the Securities and Exchange Commission (S.E.C.). Section 13 and 15 (d) of the S.E.C. Act of 1934 requires that Form 10–K be filed with the S.E.C. no later than 90 days after the close of the corporation's fiscal year. This regulation requires certain companies to submit four copies of the annual report with the 10–K.

It further states that the narrative sections of the annual report must balance with the financial data of the past fiscal year. In other words, a company cannot report the year in glowing terms in the narrative but lack the financial data to back up its optimism. Sometimes "Dear Shareholder" letters will talk about a "period of readjustment" or a "realignment of priorities." Seasoned investors know these key words mean that the chief executive officer is less than happy with the company's past performance.

Most progressive, public relations-minded corporations consider the annual report to be the most important communication to their shareholders—even if they send quarterly statements and other materials throughout the fiscal year. Because it is such a vital public relations tool, it is well worth the planning and effort needed to produce a creditable report, both well written and designed.

Some management personnel contend that as long as an investor receives a dividend each quarter, the investor cares nothing about the company or its propaganda. Most people, however, believe that anyone investing money in a company will be interested in how that company does business. As such, the annual report projects the personality and quality of the corporation's management: progressive, conservative, or somewhere in between. Part of that impression results from the design of the report, meaning its use of design (color, photographs, illustrations, graphs) and its treatment of the text (boastful, overly modest, sincerely objective).

Production of the annual report

In preparing the report, you will not deal with the financial data as such (the profit and loss statement, the balance sheet, etc.), but you will write the copy from information given you and you will help with the layout of the graphics, charts, and tables.

As the *Wall Street Journal* once wryly pointed out, most reports sound as if they were written by a committee. Experienced practitioners agree, "They were." Your role will be that of a journalist, obtaining the facts from the various divisions and departments. In addition, the chief executive officer usually has ideas on what should be featured, what new product or service was launched, what new division was started, and how production and sales figures were increased (hopefully). Your objective is to use this information to accurately describe the company's operation over the past year. You will be showing how well the company did in its financial statements prepared by the auditors.

Most annual reports are written and printed before the corporation's annual meeting. There is also a deadline for the annual report to be mailed to shareholders. Because of these deadlines, ample time must be planned to write, design, and print the report. Many corporations with branches and divisions in a number of markets, domestic and international, work on the report throughout the year. At least three months should be devoted to gathering the material for the report, writing the copy, designing, collecting photos, and obtaining financial statements. You should allow time for corporate attorneys and management to approve the copy. Finally, you should budget time to print and distribute the report.

Layout

Some companies without outside or in-house artists have someone write copy, gather photos and graphs, and release the report to the printer to design and print. In these cases the printer would ask his staff artist or a freelancer to produce the report. It is preferable, however, for an in-house company employee to prepare the layout.

Production of the report can be done in several ways. You could decide on the size of the booklet, have an artist do a dummy (a mock-up replica of the book without type or illustrations) and then write the copy. Another method would be to write a rough copy draft and then have the artist do a layout, leaving room for the financial data.

Whatever the method—writing the copy first or designing the layout before the copy is written—there is a time when a dummy must be done. Most reports are in booklet form, printed and bound in four-page multiples. Sizes vary, but the standard size is eleven inches deep by eight and one-half inches wide. Reports in this size are easy to mail and may be filed in a folder or on a shelf. (Most security analysis and financial writers retain annual reports year by year.)

As previously mentioned in the chapter on brochures, the size and style of type to be used must be decided upon and told to the typesetter who will compose the material. Typesetters can provide you with books showing the various typefaces available. Choose a face that's appropriate for your subject matter. Remember that the face should be easy to read.

Some faces have serifs, small lines crossing the ends of the main strokes. Other faces are sanserif, meaning "without serifs." Serif faces are sometimes considered traditional and easy to read, such as Times Roman and Caledonia:

Times Roman   Caledonia

Sanserif faces are thought to be more simple and modern, such as Optima and Helvetica:

Optima   **Helvetica**

For contrast and interest, heading and/or charts may be in a different face or variation than the body of the copy. Some faces have variations within the face, such as bold, italic, or condensed. See Figure 4–1 for examples from the Helvetica family.

When specifying type, always provide the following information: name of face, type size and leading, type width. Variations of type size, measured in points, are shown in Figure 4–2. Nine and ten-point type are commonly used for text in books. Headings in text body range from nine point to twelve point. Title headings can be larger.

Leading (pronounced lĕding) is the space between lines. When using ten-point type, two points leading is common (for example, this text). When using twenty-four point type, six points leading can be used.

Other interesting terms include

1. *Reverse*—when the words print white on a dark background instead of using black type on a white background.

2. *Overprinting*—when words print over a light area of an illustration or photo or reverse out of a dark area of illustration.

3. *Trim*—the page dimensions.

4. *Bleed*—when the illustration extends beyond the normal margins to the trim.

5. *Halftones and screens*—Printed photographs are called halftones because they are shot through a halftone screen. The screen is a sheet of glass ruled with crossing lines forming clear boxes. A screen with many lines (110–133) provides a finely printed halftone and is used in books and magazines. (See figure 4–3.) Newspapers use 55,

Helvetica Light

Helvetica family

Helvetica Light Italic

Helvetica family

Helvetica Regular

Helvetica family

Helvetica Regular Italic

Helvetica family

Helvetica Medium

Helvetica family

Helvetica Medium Italic

Helvetica family

Helvetica Bold

Helvetica family

Helvetica Bold Italic

Helvetica family

Figure 4–1. Variations in the Helvetica type family.

SIZE of type   8 POINT

SIZE of type   10 POINT

SIZE of type   12 POINT

text type

SIZE of type   14 POINT

SIZE of type   18 POINT

SIZE of type   24 POINT

SIZE of type   30 POINT

display type

SIZE of type   36 POINT

SIZE of type   42 POINT

SIZE of type   48 POINT

Figure 4–2. Sample variations in type size.

44

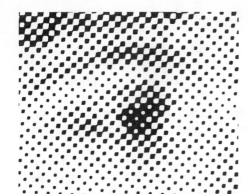

Figure 4–3.
Enlarged halftone showing the effects of screening.

65, and 85 line screens. You should tell the offset printer what line screen you want. Solid areas (type or blocks of ink) can also be screened to print lighter. Type can be screened itself, printed over a light screen, or reversed out of a dark screen. Halftones and illustrations should be cropped and marked for percent of reduction. On your copy for the printer, indicate where the halftone should go with a cornered box.

6. *Four-color*—the method for producing full-color printing. First the color artwork or photo is photographed through filters. An engraving is made for each of four basic colors: red, yellow, blue, and black. These engravings are printed separately, then superimposed on each other using transparent inks, resulting in a color-blended illustration.

Writing and organization

Shareholders demand facts; they want a clear report on how the company did during the past business year. Naturally, then, your style of writing should be factual, expository. Although some writers employ narrative combined with illustration, example, and description, factual description is by far the best style. (See an example of a clear report on pp. 47–49. This report for company employees emphasizes simple explanations about finances.)

In organization, you might find that your company—especially if it is a large corporation with international divisions—uses a consistent format every year, with such subjects as products, employees, social responsibility, foreign operations, domestic operations, and new divisions.

However, most writers will organize the text by departments, divisions, sections, branches, or subsidiaries. The importance of a department in the overall company operation dictates how much space to devote to that area. Perhaps the division is new or produced spectacular earnings; it may then receive several pages of coverage. You will want to find out what is considered important by management in order to decide how much coverage is warranted.

Here's an example of a "Dear Shareholder" letter from a plastics manufacturer:

Dear Shareholder:

During the past year, the plastic industry faced severe economic problems because of the rapidly rising inflation rate in this country. Despite this problem, Seiler Plastics Corporation had a reasonably profitable year.

1978 Employee Annual Report
Bell & Howell Company

Consumer Photo Products

Bell & Howell's Consumer Photo Products business achieved significant sales gains and increased customer acceptance in 1978 with its wide variety of high quality consumer photographic equipment under the trademark names of Bell & Howell, Mamiya and Beaulieu. The Company's 8mm cameras and projectors became the market share leaders in the United States. Mamiya medium format photographic products also strengthened as the market leader.

However, the Consumer Photo Products business again reported losses for 1978 due to low margins. Although these losses were not as severe as those of 1977, the Company has accelerated its cost reduction program.

Early in 1979 Bell & Howell introduced a consumer sound movie camera which incorporates a new automatic focusing feature. Also in 1979, the Company will introduce a new silent movie camera with a lens complement that allows zoom lens picture-taking without movie lights at a very attractive price.

Bell & Howell's innovative Slide Cube projector remained a major factor in the still photography field. Mamiya medium format cameras and accessories continued to achieve market share gains, sparked by the revolutionary new M645 product line. The M645 system produces negatives nearly three times the size of 35mm negatives for superior quality enlargements; yet the M645 has the handling ease of a 35mm camera.

The Optics Division, a leader in optical technology, continued to build its base of government and commercial contract business. Production of the M-19 military binocular was initiated and the division received a U.S. Army development contract for low cost night vision goggles.

Mamiya medium format cameras achieved market share gains in 1978. This Mamiya M645 1000S offers such features as interchangeable viewfinders and focusing screens; power drive, automatic film advance; and AE (automatic exposure) viewfinder.

The SoundStar super 8 movie camera is equipped with power zoom lens, and fast, low-light lenses for shooting in natural light.

Courtesy of Bell & Howell Co.

47

How We Distributed Revenues

Balance Sheet
(dollars in thousands)

	1978	1977
Assets (We Own)		
Cash to pay bills	$ 8,514	$ 4,409
Money invested in marketable securities	—	18,313
Money due from customers	136,122	110,389
Land, buildings and equipment (less depreciation)	64,165	63,837
Inventories	134,476	137,591
Expenses and taxes which we prepaid	8,079	6,674
Miscellaneous assets	31,087	29,348
Total	$382,443	$370,561

	1978	1977
Liabilities (We Owe) and Shareholders' Assets		
Money owed to suppliers, banks and others we must pay soon	$98,375	$70,218
Money borrowed from banks and other lenders to be paid in the future	62,399	55,714
Services we owe to others for which we have been or will be paid in cash	14,710	14,377
Taxes we must pay soon	6,164	35,786
Taxes we must pay in the future	10,117	8,628
Miscellaneous liabilities	4,593	4,104
Total	196,358	188,827
Leaving shareholders' assets of	186,085	181,734
Which is divided into:		
Money shareholders have invested by buying common and preferred stock	35,658	38,729
Amount paid by shareholders over the par value of each share	13,975	13,975
Earnings put back into the business	136,452	129,030
Total liabilities added to shareholders' assets	$382,443	$370,561

Summary of Income and Earnings

(dollars in thousands)

	1978	1977
Sales to customers	$567,523	$491,570
Interest and other income	4,252	2,675
Expenses for wages, salaries, benefits	233,469	215,943
Raw materials, research, marketing, administration and other expenses	318,967	255,728
Which left our income before taxes	19,339	22,574
After providing for taxes of	7,059	10,992
Which left earnings from operations of	12,280	11,582
Then, we took our earnings invested in the business at the beginning of the year	129,030	122,275
And paid dividends to shareholders on preferred stock, $2.50 per share	22	22
on common stock, $.87 per share in 1978 and $.84 per share in 1977	4,836	4,805
Which left us reinvested in the business at the end of the year	$136,452	$129,030

Affirmative Action

Bell & Howell recognizes that our most valuable resource is our people, and we are committed to ensuring continued growth and development for employees.

This commitment includes the active effort to draw new talent into the work force from all groups—men, women, minorities and handicapped individuals.

Through our Career Access Program, job posting, and educational development opportunities, Bell & Howell successfully encourages and recognizes effective performance at every level.

Adherence to our policies of equal employment opportunity and affirmative action in hiring, placement, promotion and compensation have been instrumental in developing the strength of our current work force.

Design: Perception, Inc.
Photography: Archie Lieberman
Printing: Hillison & Etten Co., a division of John Blair & Company

Earnings for the year at $3.55 per share were up marginally over last year's $3.42.

Sales demand was strong, especially during the last half of the year, and our earnings were up 27 percent over the previous year.

All our international divisions—England, Ireland, India, Germany, Australia, and Japan—showed a profit. Our new division in New Zealand is expected to start operation within a year.

During the year we welcomed to the Board of Directors, Nelson S. Rubin, president of Rubin Manufacturing; Harrison K. Pierce, president of WES National Bank; and Robert N. Noton, M.D.

William Ellis

William Ellis, president

Production

The Seiler Plastics Corporation, with its four manufacturing plants in this country, doubled its output last year.

This record production was due to new technology in the manufacture of plastic and the adding of a third shift in three of our four domestic plants.

With our high production rate, we were able to stockpile our plastic and ship all sales orders within two weeks. This new method is a marked improvement. We were not always able to ship orders on a current basis in previous years. We feel it important to be able to ship to our regular customers within two weeks of an order.

Marketing

The Marketing Division has offices in all the plastic centers of this country, as well as in the free world. Our sales force works directly for the Seiler Plastics Corporation, and an additional force of manufacturers' representatives represent us in a number of industries.

Our plastic is sold to the major manufacturing industries throughout the world, including manufacturers of automobiles, electrical appliances, and communication equipment. Our plastic is used by a number of small industries and these are covered by our manufacturers' representatives.

Sales are up 27 percent over last year. The automobile industry, here and foreign, represents a major portion of that substantial increase.

International

The Seiler Plastics Corporation has operating plants in six foreign countries, and the New Zealand plant, now under construction, is expected to be operational within a year.

The corporation now can supply customers in the free world within a matter of weeks instead of months. Foreign markets sales represent 40 percent of sales; as such, plants must be located near customers.

Customers can be supplied at competitive prices, and many of our domestic customers, especially those in the automobile industry, have plants throughout the world.

It is for this reason that the new plant in New Zealand is being built; three of our major customers now have plants there, and shipments must be expedited to those plants.

The plant at Bellingham, England (the first foreign plant of the company, now twenty years old) last year doubled its output to meet an increase in sales in that country. The Seiler Plastics Corporation now is the sole supplier of plastic for a large English manufacturer.

Personnel

The Seiler Plastics Corporation, with 58,000 employees here and in foreign countries, is aware of its role as an employer. Our company benefit program includes a pension plan, full medical and dental insurance , and special educational incentive programs. Equal opportunity employment continues to be a priority.

The text of this annual report is brief and to the point. The copy understates the corporation's performance, as the management felt the profitability of the company, with an increased dividend, supported the advisability of investment.

Full-color photographs of all the plants, here and abroad, complete with captions, illustrate the text in addition to photographs of the executive officers, directors, and plant managers.

The front cover shows in color the corporation headquarters. Out of the sixteen total text pages (not including the cover) eight pages detail financial data.

The larger the corporation, the more the annual report has to cover. Your challenge is to keep it concise and interesting. One large commercial bank, with an international division, issued a seventy-two-page annual report, with eighteen pages of text, including an ample supply of photographs and forty-five-pages of financial data. The remainder of the book listed officers, board of directors, and other personnel information.

To illustrate the organization of a large report, here is a brief outline of the bank's report text: 1. The Chairman of the Board and the President both signed the opening stockholders' letter. The divisions were listed as Commercial, Correspondent, Factoring and Commercial Financing, Leasing, Real Estate, International, Venture Capital, Subsidiary Banks, Investments and Money Market Operations, Personal Banking, Check Verification, Trust and Investment, Shareholder Services, Cash Management, Deposit Operations, Law Office, Personnel, and Development. Including the letter, this text took nine pages. 2. Photographs of the board of directors, listed in alphabetic order, took two pages. 3. The writer devoted ten pages to a special section, "Automation Comes of Age." It gave an overview of a cross section of "services that have brought us new customers and enabled us to expand our market." The text gave one paragraph to each of these automated services, each illustrated with a color photograph. The services were custody, dividend reinvestment, corporate trusteeship, mutual funds, pension trust, correspondent banking, bank processing, facilities management, concentration service, automated financial accounting, freight payment, payroll, export promotion, lock box, check collection, national check transmission, international collections, factoring, and financing and account reconciliation.

Reports for nonprofit groups

Most nonprofit organizations (schools, hospitals, foundations) issue annual reports. Although these organizations do not have stockholders, they do have contributors. Their reports are basically for those people who support the organization not only as financial contributors but as volunteers. Such reports contain audited financial statements showing income (including donations) and how the funds were spent. Although not regulated federally, these organizations are governed by state regulations. Those organizations receiving federal funds or research must report annually to the appropriate federal agency.

Nonprofit organizations must be aware of their responsibility to the public in reporting services rendered for the year. Most of the reports are factual, the design and text reflecting the manner in which the organization is operated and what specific public needs it meets.

Hospitals issue reports annually to tell the community it serves how they have met the medical needs of the community residents. Here's a sample annual report:

Dear Friend:

The following pages give a department-by-department look at the operation of the Riverview Hospital during the past year.

We feel we have made significant strides both in the patient care and in the modernization of our physical plant.

The cost of medical care still is rising; and although we are trying to keep costs down, we cannot compromise patient care and treatment. Our high medical standards must be maintained.

The question of the continuation of our nursing school has not been resolved. We decided to continue the school for another year, but if the school cannot be operated without a substantial deficit, we will be forced to close it.

Our nursing school is nearly fifty years old and we very much regret this move, but unfortunately we must if the school's finances do not improve. Unfortunately, a number of other community hospitals face the same situation.

In October, Dr. Harrison L. Brown retired as chief of staff, a position he held for two decades. Dr. Brown's distinguished medical career spans more than half a century. His contributions to the growth of Riverview Hospital are innumerable. We are delighted to note that Dr. Brown, although retired, will continue as a consultant to the medical staff.

Lawrence Hilton
Administrator

Surgery

Two new operating suites were constructed last year to relieve the need for more space. We now have five fully equipped operating rooms, including one suite that is kept open for emergency procedures.

A total of 4,321 surgical procedures were performed by members of our surgical staff last year. This is a significant increase of 25 percent over the previous year.

One of the giant steps taken by the Surgical Department was our first coronary bypass surgery. Although open-heart surgery is not new, previously these complex procedures were done in teaching hospitals and medical centers.

As surgical techniques and knowledge have expanded, the surgical staff believed that such procedures could be performed successfully at Riverview. The first such procedure was performed successfully in April. Several others are now scheduled.

Medical

The medical department has increased its bed capacity for 25 and has now a total of 125. The need for more nonsurgical beds was apparent in March when a flu epidemic filled the wards.

Two new wards were activated and at the medical staff's request, continued. The Board of Trustees approved this measure.

Outpatient

With the dramatic increase in population of our community in the past five years, especially with the opening of three new industries, the need for daily outpatient clinics became apparent.

A medical committee was formed two years ago to study this problem. They recommended that six clinics be started.

A year ago, three local companies contributed a total of $100,000 to construct and operate these six clinics, each staffed by a group of specialists.

The clinics were opened last January and this year 4,567 patients used the facilities. The new clinics work in the areas of pediatrics; speech and hearing; cardiac; ear, nose, and throat; cancer; and nutrition.

Two other clinics, working in gynecology and arthritis, will be opened this January. If funds can be obtained, another clinic in psychiatry will open in September.

Accident Ward

Riverview has a contract with the town to supply medical and accident services. Our accident ward is open twenty-four hours a day and handles all types of medical and accident emergencies. The ward's medical staff treated 4,213 patients last year.

Radiology

The radiology department was expanded last year to include a new X ray for diagnostic purposes. The department is an integral part of the hospital's operation, not only in diagnostic work but in therapy as well.

Pathology

The pathology department was reorganized last year, with Dr. Martin N. Burgin as pathologist-in-chief. A total of 4,358,234 tests were conducted by the department.

Volunteers

Volunteers have always been a great aid in the day-by-day operation of Riverview. Their services are invaluable. Last year our 324 volunteers provided 12,476 hours of service to the hospital.

Although traditionally volunteers have been women, last year twelve men volunteered their time and talents to the hospital.

These men, retired from their business and professional careers, have volunteered for a number of jobs, including the much-needed manning of the information desk (especially weekends and holidays) and of the business office.

The Ladies' Volunteer Committee is in charge of the gift shop, the patients' cart, and the visitors' coffee shop. All profits from the sale of gifts and food is donated to the hospital for special patient projects, such as providing entertainment on holdiays.

Housekeeping

The Housekeeping Department's responsibility is twofold. Not only does the department's personnel (janitors and maids) clean the plant's interior (an ongoing process), other personnel operate the hospital's laundry.

Buildings and Grounds

The care and maintenance of the hospital's five buildings and fourteen acres of land, including the 100-car parking lot, is the responsibility of the buildings and grounds department. All construction personnel —carpenters, masons, painters, plumbers, plasterers, and electricians —are represented in the department. Other employees include ground-keepers, gardeners, and snowplow operators.

Security

The security force includes fourteen full-time and twelve part-time men. A seven-day, twenty-four-hour security officer now guards the buildings and the grounds.

In this report, the administrator's letter sets the tone for the information to follow by warning the readers of rising medical costs and the unresolved question of the nursing school. This information is vital to the readers, who are the users and financial supporters of the hospital.

In writing style and layout, the emphasis is on facts and clarity. The content, which is low key, is presented in nontechnical language with nonposed photos of daily hospital routine. In addition, there are several photos of the accident floor personnel in action and the cover features a male volunteer at the information desk. The information within the report is modest. For example, open-heart surgery is mentioned in the third paragraph. While it is called a "giant step," the tone is factual, not overly dramatic.

In organization, there are several segments. First, the letter; next, the listing of departments. Note how the mention of volunteers bridges the gap between patient care and in-house departments. Each department needn't be listed every year in the text of the report, although usually all patient-care departments merit at least a paragraph. For example, in this report, two departments, records and kitchen, were not listed. They could be next year.

The report includes the names of all members of the medical staff, visiting and attending surgeons and physicians, department heads of the nonmedical departments, and the board of trustees.

Finally, financial statements and data are in the back of the book. The report totals 16 pages, including the cover.

A medical center or teaching hospital uses a similar format to the one previously illustrated, with an introductory letter by the administrator or president of the board of trustees. The text reports the accomplishments of each department, and its style is more technical and medically sophisticated.

Such reports focus on the decision makers of government agencies, funds, and foundations. These people decide on what grants to give for research, patient care, and other projects.

To illustrate, here's a brief excerpt from the report of Newman Medical Center. They wrote an overall story on grant monies for their report.

An analysis of the sources of support for research, training, and sponsored clinical programs shows a significant increase ($1.2 million) over the past year.

The Department of Health, Education, and Welfare (HEW) continues to provide the majority of support, 69 percent. It increased approximately $300,000.

Some highlights: The Myerson Foundation's grant of $78,908 for an examination of the current state-of-the-art in cognitive development of infants; the National Milk Council's grant of $32,890 to study the effect of lactobacillus feeding on intestinal bacterial enzymes; the Norton Research Fund's grant of $67,456 to study the effectiveness of counterpulsation; and a grant of $45,678 from various drug companies for a research project on evaluating amyotrophic lateral sclerosis.

The Grants Administration Office processed 123 applications for funding; 29 of those were continuation requests. Of the remaining applications, more than 51 percent were funded by various grantors.

This excerpt is right to the point. The writer assumes the readers are medically and research oriented.

Summary

Profit and nonprofit corporations produce annual reports to show the public their records over the past year. The practitioner selects the appropriate information to report objectively the performance. These reports are vital to the organization's public information program, playing a unique role in public relations.

5

Public relations and institutional advertising

When public relations started to bloom after World War II, a practitioner would not have considered buying space in a newspaper or magazine or time on radio or television to communicate a message. He left those areas to his colleague in marketing communications, advertising. As time passed and the pace of marketing communications increased, both public relations and advertising borrowed techniques from each other. Now in some companies it is difficult to know where advertising starts and public relations ends, especially in those companies in a noncompetitive field.

The simple difference is that while advertising sells products and services, public relations changes or reaffirms attitudes or opinions about an issue, an organization, or a company. The advertiser communicates to a market, either a geographic one or a certain defined cross section of the population (the youth market, the middle-aged market, the young-married market). In contrast, the practitioner communicates information to a large or small public (or a group of publics) who are concerned with an issue or who should be concerned.

However, they are alike in that they both communicate to people through newspapers, TV, or booklets. Each attempts to influence the audience to act or form an opinion. The advertiser says, "Buy my product, it will help you." The practitioner says, "This is the reason we think this way; please support us."

For example, many utility companies run campaigns on saving energy, saying that the rising cost of energy is the concern of both corporation and consumer. The new campaigns include tips on conservation. Just a few years ago, the campaigns promoted the use of additional energy through the sale of new hot water heaters, furnaces, and appliances. Now their goal is to win the public's empathy, if not sympathy. They want the consumer to understand the company's unfortunate plight; it is not the company's fault that there is an energy crisis.

Likewise, national oil companies use advertising techniques in public relations. Their campaigns tell of the company's ceaseless search for new oil sources and graphically depict the high cost and risks of ocean exploration.

Institutional advertising

Although the terms *public relations* and *institutional advertising* mean essentially the same thing, a distinction between the two can be made for discussion purposes. Institutional or corporate-image advertising promotes the company rather than its products or services. Public relations or advocacy advertising goes a step beyond in that it attempts to inform about a problem or concern and explain what is being done to help.

Institutional advertising certainly is not new. A review of newspapers and magazines in the early 1900s reveals various ads promoting the company rather than selling. Such ads usually try to communicate that the company is a good corporate citizen or that it cares about its employees, the environment, and its customers.

Both you and management together should decide when to advertise instead of relying on traditional publicity methods. Situations vary, of course, but a good rule is that when the media fails to tell your group's side of the story, advertise.

For example, a union calls a strike. The local news media cover the strike but don't detail why workers are striking. They simply report that it is a wage dispute. Management feels it has made a fair offer to the workers, but the union membership has rejected it, feeling that the offer does not cover the higher cost of living. Although both management and union officials have distributed news releases and spoken with newspeople, they both feel "our side of the story" is not being told.

So the company buys space in the newspaper and prints its side. The union follows suit and tells its side. Both attempt to have the residents of the community understand the issue. Because they felt it important that the public understand, they both bought space to accomplish this communications goal.

Producing a newspaper ad

The format of most newspapers, whether it be a mass circulation daily or a small community daily or weekly, is the same. Most have separate sections for news, features, sports, and display and classified advertising.

Size and placement of the ad. A standard-sized newspaper page has eight columns and 300 agate lines to a column. (See Figure 5–1.) The new technology of computer type setting and offset printing has changed some "standard" newspapers to six columns, others to five.

Before writing copy, decide how large the ad will be. Indicate the column width in number of columns and the depth in number of lines.

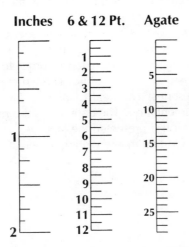

Inches   6 & 12 Pt.   Agate

Figure 5–1. Agate measurement.

Because there are 14 lines to the column inch, the typesetter and pasteup person know what size the ad is by your information of width and depth. For example, a three-column by 50-line ad has a total of 150 lines, 50 lines to each column. Thus the copy would be typeset to fit into that size ad. Most ads run ROP, meaning run-of-paper. ROP ads can be placed anywhere in the newspaper at the editor's option. The advertiser cannot dictate placement in the paper. If there is an important reason for the ad to appear in a certain section, the advertiser can pay a premium charge. Although the advertiser may request a section for the placement of an ad without being charged an additional fee, he has no guarantee it will appear there.

Writing ad copy

In preparing ads, copywriters often follow the formula AIDA—attention, interest, desire, and action. To stimulate attention and desire, headlines should be provocative. The copywriter usually puts a benefit in each headline; he tells the reader how this product or service will benefit his or her life.

To promote interest, copywriters choose illustrations and photos to dress up the ad. However, such illustrations seldom appear in public relations ads, where the format usually consists of a headline, body copy, and company logo (a distinctive design of the company's name or product line).

Most importantly, the text (body copy) is editorial in style, factual. Because the goal is persuasion—action by the reader—the copy is serious.

Mobil (see Figure 5–2) is a strong practitioner of advertising public relations. Its series on a national energy policy is an excellent example of a company buying newspaper space in order to get its views read and hopefully understood by the public. The writing style in this ad, as in the others of the series, *The Real Challenge: Increasing Energy Supply,* is editorial/argumentation. The copy treats the reader as intelligent, able to form an opinion if presented the facts. Remember that how you treat the reader is important in any writing, especially in public relations advertising.

The medium

Usually the goal of the message dictates the selection of what medium to use. In the Mobil ad, newspapers are preferred, because its text is fairly

1. Should U.S. energy policy discourage coal mining?

A cynical observer recently said: "There are only two problems with coal. You can't dig it and you can't burn it."

Unfortunately, even though coal is America's most abundant energy source, there's more than a grain of truth in that comment. On the one hand, the Administration has set a goal of 1.2 billion tons of coal production a year by 1985, up from 660 million tons mined last year. But, as we'll discuss in a moment, environmental impediments strewn in the way of coal development and coal use make achievement of that goal difficult.

Which is a real waste, because the coal is there. Just from reserves already identified, America has enough coal to last 400 years at current rates of production. And coal is rich in energy potential; a ton of coal has three times the *BTU*s of a barrel of oil.

If the coal is there, why isn't it being mined?

As with most energy matters, there's no simple answer. For one thing, all coal isn't alike. Eastern coal, which is produced mostly from underground mines in states like Kentucky, West Virginia, and Pennsylvania and accounts for 80 percent of current U.S. production, is generally high in sulfur. Under proposed environmental regulations it may not be burned unless costly desulfurization equipment is installed by the user. Much western coal, which can be surface-mined, is low in sulfur. But the West, with half America's coal resources, produces only about 20 percent of current supply. Environmental restrictions against surface-mining make it time consuming to increase production. Today, it takes a minimum of two years to obtain all the permits necessary to start building a new mine.

With environmental compromises, the West could substantially boost its coal production. Unfortunately, the pressures in Washington are in the opposite direction: toward even stiffer controls on surface-mining that would make new western coal difficult to bring into production. In the East, increasing production will be extremely difficult if not impossible. Many of the mines are old, and much new capital would be required to open new ones. In addition, there simply aren't enough trained miners available.

Adding a "catch-22" touch is the controversy over that "scrubbing" equipment to remove sulfur. The Administration's proposed energy program mandates that most coal-burning utilities install the scrubbers, at a cost that could reach $50 billion. They're necessary for meeting clean-air standards if high-sulfur coal is burned, but unneeded to burn low-sulfur western coal. Unless a compromise is reached, the consumer will have to foot the bill for equipment that will often be totally irrelevant.

Needed to resolve the coal dilemma is a look at the realities of modern surface-mining. Most proposed mine sites in states like Wyoming are located on open prairie, far from centers of population. Modern surface-mining techniques carefully set aside topsoil and subsoil that is removed by the giant shovels, so the land can be restored to its original contours as each tract is mined.

Modern surface-mining, in short, is hardly the bogeyman it's made out to be. But it's a convenient scapegoat for those who seem to prefer energy shortages to making decisions favoring energy development. Coal has great potential; but unless the current drift of national energy policy is changed, much of what President Carter hopes for will remain in the ground.

We urge that the national energy debate focus on the paramount issue: development vs. non-development of U.S. energy supplies. We believe that any adverse social and economic consequences of development are being grossly over-estimated by many in Washington and that, the adverse social and economic consequences of non-development are being grossly *under*-estimated.

Mobil™

©1977 Mobil Corporation

Courtesy of Mobil Corporation.

Figure 5–2. Mobil use of editorial/argumentation style.

long. It can be read and if necessary, reread. A broadcast of thirty or sixty seconds would not allow Mobil enough time for forceful advocacy of the issues. The following discussion introduces the various media and how each operates.

Newspapers

As previously mentioned, newspapers have specific circulation areas, a factor which is excellent for the practitioner who must reach a certain geographic area with a message. Circulation figures of established newspapers are accurate; these figures are sworn to by the publisher.

Radio

Radio is an excellent advertising medium because its various programming formats (top 40, middle-of-the-road, talk, all news, country and western, religious) provide specific listener demographics. Since the station's broadcast area is easy to find out, you'll know exactly what audience listens to a station.

You will need to decide if these listeners are the ones to reach with a message. Then you can purchase several time segments or spots in one time period.

The better the station's ratings (number of listeners) the more the station charges per commercial (advertising) message. Various time segments (called *morning drive, housewife, early afternoon,* and *afternoon drive*) are priced differently. Morning drive time is more expensive per spot than housewife time, for example, because more people listen on their way to work than at midmorning.

When buying broadcast spots, keep in mind that your message must be run several times at least to make an impression. Radio primarily is a background medium; usually the listener is doing something else. You will need to buy a series of spots to be sure the message is heard. Studies show that it takes a minimum of four or five repeats for the content to be fully understood.

Most radio stations do not place commercials back-to-back, one after another. On these stations, a commercial can stand alone. The so-called "good music" or background stations are the exceptions. These stations, mostly FM, play fifteen minutes of continuous music and then break for three or four commercials in a row. This format makes it difficult for the average listener to recall which commercial said what.

Stations sell sixty and thirty seconds to advertisers; some even push ten-second spots. Because public relations advertising is serious in nature, a sixty-second spot gives the time needed to make a point.

You can write approximately 165 words for a sixty-second spot and approximately 75 words for a thirty-second spot. These limits are approximations—your spot may be two or three words under or over.

Because radio is a listening medium, writers frequently use incomplete sentences in radio commercials. Think of a radio spot as someone in a conversation, and before writing, listen to how people talk in everyday life. In radio, listeners see through their ears. As such, you'll want to build a word picture that the listener can "see."

A professional *voice* (or *talent*) usually records the message on tape if the commercial is to be used in a number of stations. This method assures the good quality of the reading of the message over each station. If no tape is provided, staff announcers at each station read the copy. When you decide on the technicalities of the presentation, pay close attention to your budget.

Here's an example of a sixty-second spot:

NEW ENGLAND'S OLDEST INDUSTRY MIGHT BECOME
EXTINCT. THE FISHING INDUSTRY CANNOT COMPETE
AGAINST FOREIGN FISHING FLEETS CLOSE TO OUR SHORES.
EXPERTS ESTIMATE THESE FLEETS, COMPLETE WITH THEIR
MANUFACTURING SHIP, WILL "FISH OUT" OUR WATERS
WITHIN FIVE YEARS. THIS MEANS THAT OUR FISHING
INDUSTRY WILL NOT BE ABLE TO OPERATE AS IT HAS SINCE
THIS COUNTRY WAS FOUNDED. THIS ALSO MEANS YOU
WILL NOT BE ABLE TO BUY FRESH FISH IN NEW ENGLAND
MARKETS. THERE WILL BE NO MORE FISH FROM THE WATERS
OF THE ATLANTIC OCEAN OFF THE COAST OF NEW
ENGLAND. A BILL NOW IN CONGRESS WOULD KEEP
FOREIGN FISHING SHIPS 200 MILES FROM OUR SHORE. THIS
BILL, NOW IN A HOUSE COMMITTEE, MUST BE BROUGHT TO
THE HOUSE FLOOR FOR QUICK APPROVAL. WRITE YOUR
CONGRESSMAN NOW. ASK THAT HE SUPPORT AND VOTE
FOR HOUSE BILL 2332. ACT NOW. SAVE NEW ENGLAND'S
OLDEST INDUSTRY FROM FOREIGN INVASION.

This sixty-second commercial contains 148 words. Its first sentence, "New England's oldest industry might become extinct," attempts to catch the listener's immediate attention. The message then explains the problem and what action resolves the problem. It asks the listener to act. The advantage of the minute commercial is that it "warms up" the listener. He or she has an opportunity to "tune in" on the copy because the message is longer and because the main theme, the threat of the foreign fleet, is repeated. When the message requests the listener to act, the problem will be understood. Compare the sixty-second message with this thirty-second spot:

> NEW ENGLAND'S OLDEST INDUSTRY MIGHT BECOME
> EXTINCT. IT'S FISHING FLEET CANNOT COMPETE AGAINST
> FOREIGN FLEETS. EXPERTS ESTIMATE FOREIGNERS WILL "FISH
> OUT" OUR WATERS WITHIN FIVE YEARS. THE FISHING
> INDUSTRY WILL BE DEAD AND FRESH FISH FROM THE
> ATLANTIC OCEAN WILL BE A THING OF THE PAST IN OUR
> MARKETS. CONGRESS IS CONSIDERING A BILL TO KEEP
> FOREIGN FISHERMEN 200 MILES FROM OUR SHORE. ASK
> YOUR CONGRESSMAN TO VOTE FOR BILL 2332.

This thirty-second commercial contains seventy-three words. Although it essentially says the same thing—that the listener should contact his or her congressman—its considerably tighter. Only an intent listener could understand the thirty-second commercial. If he or she were not paying attention to the message, the commercial would be over before the listener realized what the message was.

Television

To the advertiser, television is exciting—and expensive. For much of the public, television viewing is a way of life. Thus TV is extremely valuable to the practitioner who needs to convey a message to a large segment of the general public.

Cost. Television spots' costs vary with different time segments. The more people watching, the more the spot costs. Television time segments break down roughly to early morning, housewife (midmorning), noon, early afternoon, afternoon, early evening, family, prime, and late evening. Prime time, considered by most advertisers as eight P.M. to eleven P.M., is the most expensive.

Television production costs also can be high, especially those commercials produced for network television. With a technical crew, film and sound crew, light experts, a director, and talent, the production cost of a thirty-second spot is thousands of dollars. However, a local advertiser, running on one or two stations, usually shoots the spot at a local station or production house and the cost is considerably less.

Production. Most public relations advertising is serious in nature, such as the advocacy of one side of an issue. Whereas your spot would probably not call for elaborate production as would a nationally produced commercial selling beer, wine, or soap powder, it must look professional, not like a home movie. It will compete with the national spots for the viewer's attention. The lack of professional appeal will bother the viewer, and the effectiveness of the message will suffer.

The practitioner with a national account who buys network spots usually has a production budget to match, so he hires a production house to do the commercial. He visualizes the concept (the main theme) and the production people translate it into a commercial, starting with a storyboard and adding audio and video.

The practitioner, in thinking of a concept for the spot, first decides on one idea. Then the decision can be made on how to illustrate it. What visual method or technique will best tell the story? Simplicity is the key, both in visuals and in sound. Only thirty seconds are allowed to influence or persuade the viewer in the average TV spot; he or she must not be confused with two or three ideas. One central idea proves effective in persuading the viewer. Three other important ideas are

1. Viewers will mentally turn off the message if the first three or four seconds are dull.

2. Action holds viewers.

3. Visuals dominate sound.

For example, an oil company may shoot film of its exploration team searching for oil in the Atlantic Ocean. A utility company demonstrates how modern computers save consumer costs. A banking association shows how local banks aid the community. A national union urges the consumer to look for the union label.

Realize that what may appear to be an excellent idea in storyboards may not have impact on film. The production people should have the ability to visualize the completed spot. The director may want to add a word or two to maximize a scene's full impact. These suggestions can make a vast difference in how effective the message will be. To be the most effective in writing copy, make sure it asks these three questions:

1. What is being said?
2. Why is it being said to me?
3. What should I do about it?

Here's an example of how an automobile liability insurance companies association solved a problem. They know that the insurance rates for property damage have soared over the past four years; the rates have doubled in that period. But the public doesn't know the reason and they're angry. The media are quoting a number of elected state officials demanding an investigation into the rate-setting procedures. Some politicians hint that the insurance companies are in collusion with their rate setting.

The association knows that these accusations are false, that the real reason for the increase is that both the number of accidents and the cost of repair have doubled. This is the simple explanation, but the public's reaction continues to be hostile.

The association issues news releases explaining in detail the insurance industry's side of the controversy. Industry spokespersons appear on radio and television talk shows to answer questions. Newspaper ads are produced, tracing the increase in the number of accidents and the costs of repair.

The public relations director of the association believes a television campaign will change the public's attitude. Two concepts are considered: one has a local television personality explaining the company's position and urging driving caution, and the other shows an accident.

First both concepts are written in script form. When writing, the practitioner thinks in terms of words and pictures simultaneously. His copy paper is divided into two columns; the left-hand column is the audio, the right-hand is the video. Obviously the audio and corresponding video must relate; the audio does not talk about one point while the video is on another. The role of the audio is to interpret the picture and advance the thought. As the writer continues, he tries to visualize. He knows that some type of movement on the screen holds interest and that transitions, scene to scene, must be smooth. Too many scenes crammed into the spot will confuse the viewer.

The video description in the script (both scene and action) should be complete as possible, such as this one:

Audio	Video
I'M SAM KIRK AND I'M BOTHERED BY AUTOMOBILE INSURANCE RATES.	Man sitting behind desk, medium shot; establish office set: uncluttered background.

OUR INSURANCE RATES HAVE DOUBLED. I ASKED, WHY?	Camera comes in slowly; tight shot, head and shoulders.
THE NUMBER OF AUTOMOBILE ACCIDENTS HAVE DOUBLED FROM THREE HUNDRED THOUSAND TO SIX HUNDRED THOUSAND. AND THE COST OF REPAIRING A DAMAGED CAR HAS DOUBLED, TOO.	Man stands up behind desk; points to chart on easel to his right. Medium shot. Pan chart.
WHAT CAN YOU DO TO REDUCE COSTS? DRIVE DEFENSIVELY. PRACTICE SAFETY ON THE HIGHWAYS. IT WILL PAY OFF FOR US ALL.	Camera back to man; standing, looking straight at camera. Tight shot.
	Logo of insurance companies' association.

Production of this spot would not be expensive. Videotaped in a studio, it could be shot continuously. (Most television ads are videotaped; many of those filmed on location outside the studio also are later transferred to videotape.) Editing this tape would be at a minimum. The lighting of the man's face would be critical as there are two closeups, but otherwise it is a simple spot to produce.

Second example:

Audio	**Video**
REGULAR TRAFFIC SOUND PLUS RAIN PELTING DOWN.	Long shot of automobile on highway during rainstorm, car comes toward camera.
SKID SOUNDS, BREAKS SQUEAL, ETC. CRASH SOUND, GLASS SHATTERING, STEAM HISSING FROM ENGINE.	Medium shot: car skids on wet pavement; hits pole. Tight shot of front of damaged car.

Repairman:	Medium shot of repair
"AND THIS WILL COST NINE	shop: action in
HUNDRED AND EIGHTY-NINE	background. Come in
DOLLARS, WITH THE NEW	on repairman and
RADIATOR AND GRILL."	adjustor; frame the shot.
Adjustor:	As they inspect damage,
"COME OFF IT, WITH A NEW	cut to adjustor.
RADIATOR AND GRILL THAT	
WAS ONLY FIVE HUNDRED	
DOLLARS LAST YEAR."	
Repairman:	Cut to repairman.
"THAT WAS LAST YEAR."	
Adjustor:	Cut to adjustor.
"WHERE WILL IT END?"	
Repairman:	Cut to repairman.
"WHEN PEOPLE START TO	Logo of insurance
DRIVE SAFELY."	companies' association.

The first ten seconds of this spot show the car approach and subsequent crash. The remainder deals with the dialogue in the repairshop. Because it uses two locations to shoot and two actors, a minimum of two days would be needed to shoot and one day would be used to edit. For these reasons, production costs for the second spot would be higher than the first version.

In content, each spot could be effective. Both show that accidents and costs are up. But in comparison, the first spot has a stronger message: "What can you do to reduce costs? Drive defensively. Practice safety on the highways. It will pay off for all of us."

Public service

The Federal Communications Commission advocates that both radio and television stations provide free public service announcements (PSA) for nonprofit organizations. Thousands of foundations and organizations use the PSA to tell their story to the public. Charitable groups and all the medical foundations—including cancer, arthritis, and diabetes—provide spots to radio and television.

A foundation or organization must be nonprofit to take advantage of free spots. Stations usually cooperate with both worthy local and national foundations.

Large stations usually have one person in charge of the acceptance and scheduling of public service announcements. Director of Public Service is the general title for such an employee. On the smaller stations the regular program director selects public service spots.

National foundations (who usually have adequate production budgets) tape their spots and distribute the tapes to stations throughout the country. Station managers approve of this technique because of the generally high quality of the tapes' production. Many stations (especially FM) are automated, and taped PSA's are easy to intergrate into the broadcast day.

However, stations still use straight copy for public service announcements. The practitioner for a local nonprofit group writes the spot and sends it to the local station. The station uses the copy because the organization is within its broadcast area.

For radio, most practitioners supply a station with spots of sixty, thirty, and ten seconds so that the manager will have flexibility in scheduling.

Here's an example of a ten-second spot:

EMPLOYERS, IT IS GOOD BUSINESS TO PROVIDE ANNUAL
PHYSICAL EXAMINATIONS FOR YOUR EMPLOYEES. CALL
528–1999 FOR INFORMATION.

An example of a thirty-second spot:

EMPLOYERS, IT IS GOOD BUSINESS TO PROVIDE ANNUAL
PHYSICAL EXAMS FOR ALL YOUR EMPLOYEES ON THE
EXECUTIVE AND NONEXECUTIVE LEVEL. AS A COMMUNITY
SERVICE, THE NORTHWEST MEDICAL ASSOCIATION AIDS
COMPANIES IN ARRANGING ANNUAL PHYSICALS FOR THEIR
EMPLOYEES. MORE THAN ONE HUNDRED COMPANIES NOW
ARE PROVIDING THIS ADDITIONAL BENEFIT.. A
REPRESENTATIVE OF THE NORTHWEST MEDICAL ASSOCIATION
WILL MEET WITH YOU AND DISCUSS SUCH A PROGRAM.
CALL 528–1999 FOR MORE INFORMATION.

An example of a sixty-second spot:

EMPLOYERS, IT IS GOOD BUSINESS TO PROVIDE ANNUAL
PHYSICAL EXAMS FOR YOUR EMPLOYEES ON THE EXECUTIVE
AND NONEXECUTIVE LEVEL. THE NORTHWEST MEDICAL
ASSOCIATION, A NONPROFIT ORGANIZATION, AIDS
COMPANIES IN ARRANGING ANNUAL PHYSICALS FOR THEIR
EMPLOYEES. EXAMINATIONS CAN BE CONDUCTED AT THE
EMPLOYER'S PLACE OF BUSINESS IF THERE IS A ROOM OR AT
A CONVENIENT HOSPITAL OR CLINIC. THE PRICE FOR SUCH
EXAMINATIONS IS NOMINAL. EMPLOYEES ARE HAPPIER,
RESULTING IN HIGHER MORALE IN YOUR WORK FORCE. THE
RESULTS OF THE EXAMINATION ARE SHOWN ONLY TO THE
EMPLOYEE. AS A COMMUNITY SERVICE, THE NORTHWEST
MEDICAL ASSOCIATION WILL SEND A KNOWLEDGEABLE
REPRESENTATIVE TO DISCUSS SUCH A PROGRAM. IF YOU
WISH, THE REPRESENTATIVE THEN WILL TALK TO UNION
OFFICIALS OR EMPLOYEE REPRESENTATIVES, ANSWERING ANY
QUESTIONS. THIS CAN BE A GIANT STEP IN YOUR
EMPLOYEES' BENEFIT PROGRAM. CALL THE NORTHWEST
MEDICAL ASSOCIATION AT 528–1999 FOR MORE
INFORMATION. THAT NUMBER AGAIN IS 528–1999. NO
COMPANY IS EITHER TOO LARGE OR TOO SMALL FOR SUCH
A PROGRAM.

Production techniques in the shooting of public service spots have improved during the last ten years along with the making of regular commercials. The National Advertising Council contributes its members' talents in aiding national foundations to produce television spots. Many practitioners can hire production people to create and produce a message.

If you have little or no budget, you need not despair, because at times local stations shoot a PSA for a local group as a community service. In these cases, you write the spot, make a suggestion or two on the video side, and the station's production crew takes it from there. You can provide slides to be used on the screen while the copy is being read. For example, a thirty-second spot about annual examinations might be done this way on little or no budget:

Audio	Video
EMPLOYERS, IT IS GOOD BUSINESS TO PROVIDE ANNUAL PHYSICAL EXAMS FOR EMPLOYEES, BOTH EXECUTIVE AND NONEXECUTIVE.	*Slide 1*—Photo of employees in a work situation.
AS A COMMUNITY SERVICE, THE NORTHWEST MEDICAL ASSOCIATION AIDS COMPANIES IN ARRANGING ANNUAL PHYSICAL EXAMINATIONS FOR THEIR EMPLOYEES.	*Slide 2*—Man or woman talking to physician in white lab coat at desk.
MORE THAN ONE HUNDRED COMPANIES NOW PROVIDE SUCH EXAMINATIONS.	*Slide 3*—Man having an EKG or some other medical test.
A REPRESENTATIVE OF THE NORTHWEST MEDICAL ASSOCIATION WILL MEET WITH YOU TO DISCUSS SUCH A PROGRAM. CALL 528–1999 FOR MORE INFORMATION.	*Slide 4*—Telephone number.

This same spot could be shot on film with a "voice-over" technique on audio. The announcer reads the spot while the film runs (see p. 74).

Film production costs would be inexpensive for this last spot and the spot would still be effective. Film experts say that each scene should last at least four seconds because it takes the viewer that long to comprehend the scene. Cutting from one scene to another too rapidly confuses the viewer; the impact of the message in the spot would be lost.

Basically, then, practitioners employ the same techniques in writing public service spots for radio and television as they do in writing public relations advertising. Focus on one central idea or theme and

Audio	Video
EMPLOYERS, IT IS GOOD BUSINESS TO PROVIDE ANNUAL PHYSICAL EXAMS FOR EMPLOYEES, BOTH EXECUTIVE AND NONEXECUTIVE. AS A COMMUNITY SERVICE, THE NORTHWEST MEDICAL ASSOCIATION AIDS COMPANIES IN ARRANGING ANNUAL PHYSICAL EXAMINATIONS FOR THEIR EMPLOYEES. MORE THAN ONE HUNDRED COMPANIES NOW PROVIDE SUCH EXAMINATIONS.	Shot of men and women working in a modern factory. Medium shot of workers on line with machines. Busy scene, lots of activity; come in close on one employee intently working, might be working on a bread board (electronic circuit board).
A REPRESENTATIVE OF THE NORTHWEST MEDICAL ASSOCIATION WILL MEET WITH YOU TO DISCUSS SUCH A PROGRAM. CALL 528–1999 FOR MORE INFORMATION.	*New scene*: Employees going through examination; physician talking to patient; several random shots of exam, etc. Telephone number slide (*five seconds*)

then expand on it, employing the AIDA formula (attention, interest, desire, action).

Summary

Advertising techniques are used in some public relations campaigns to inform the public about a problem or concern. Usually, the goal of the message dictates the selection of the medium. Radio and television offer free public service announcements (PSA) to nonprofit organizations. Stations use local and national PSA and no matter what the budget for broadcast production, a practitioner can usually obtain broadcast time for a worthy nonprofit organization.

Speech writing

Most organizations—both profit and nonprofit—actively solicit speaking engagements among clubs and community groups. Utility companies are a case in point. A practitioner for such a company tries to reach all the clubs and organizations in the company's marketing area to supply speakers at regular meetings. These speeches give the company a chance to tell its side of controversial issues, such as raises in rates. In other examples, a practitioner for a local hospital might speak about services to the community. A trade association's practitioner might seek out business organizations or clubs as a way to tell his industry's story.

You may find it helpful to organize a speaker's bureau of volunteers from your organization. You then match the speaking engagement with the member of the speaker's bureau best fitted for that assignment. The president of the company may speak at an important meeting, while a vice-president may be assigned to speak at a PTA meeting.

You'll write the speeches for the members of the group. The importance of the meeting to the organization dictates your role not only in writing the speech but in helping the speaker at the meeting. (At times you will deliver the speech, but usually a member of the bureau is better.) Helpful things you can do include checking out the loudspeaker system. The speaker should stand about a foot away from the microphone and you can check this. You can also turn up the amplifier to gain control to a point higher than it would be normally because meeting rooms are more sound-absorptive when filled.

Most speakers, even those with experience, are somewhat nervous. You can make it easier for the speaker in several ways. If the speaker is not on the podium at the time he or she is scheduled to speak, find the easiest way to get to the stand, such as a side door. Make sure the notes being used to introduce your speaker are accurate and up-to-date.

Writing style

Speech writing differs from writing for print in that the material will be heard, not read.

Before writing, think about these factors:

What does the audience know already about the subject?

How would it be possible to demonstrate that the subject is really important?

Will the audience be in favor of, opposed to, or undecided about the subject?

Use the answers to these questions to decide what type of focus to give your speech. Write to fit your audience's level of understanding and interest. Remember that you can't cover a subject thoroughly if you only have four or five minutes, so being concise is important.

Like brochures, informational speeches use details and examples in a narrative style. Many expert speech writers feel a good example in a speech is far more persuasive than the most cogent of arguments. If you make generalizations, qualify and support them. If using source materials, note authorities; in this way you demonstrate that those reputable in the field believe as the speaker does; this strengthens your case.

If the speech deals with a controversial subject, then recognize all the evidence, both pro and con. Such a speech recognizes the truth on both sides, respecting honest opinions that differ.

When you use statistics, translate the figures into round numbers. Percentages or fractions provide more impact than actual figures because they present a clearer idea of proportion. Along this line, try to make all evidence as vivid as possible, using a word picture. A colorful analogy or an anecdote in the form of an analogy may be incorporated to bring a point home dramatically.

Structure

Once you know the topic and focus of the speech, organize the material so that both speaker and audience can follow it easily. The pattern must be simpler than in a brochure; realize that the audience must absorb ideas throughout the speech. For example, in a speech of five or six minutes, make only two or three specific points. More ideas than this will confuse the audience; they'll miss the main idea.

Three basic factors determine the structure of a speech: your subject, the audience, and your purpose. In the next few pages we'll discuss how these relate to the four basic speech structures: supporting a generalization, key words, question and answer, and problem solving.

Supporting a generalization

Outlining a generalization structure is easy. First state the generalization and then offer supporting evidence, including examples, descriptive details, and analogies. In other words, tell them what you are going to tell them; then tell them; and finally tell them what you told them. The speech follows a logical pattern. For example, here's a speech presented to a group of workers:

> You have been discriminated against when you tried to get a job. You file a complaint with the U.S. Equal Employment Opportunity Commission. Who knows, it might be resolved in 1985. That is, if you're lucky.
>
> It takes the job discrimination agency two years to settle the average bias complaint. There are 13,000 such cases piled up at the Commission now. By the end of next year, the unresolved backlog is likely to reach 162,000.
>
> Franklin K. is an example. Over 50, he applied for a job as advertising manager for an insurance company. The company advertised for a mature individual with experience in insurance advertising.
>
> Franklin read the ad in a trade publication and submitted his resumé. He knew it was difficult to land a job after 50, so he was careful to cut a few years here and there on the resumé.

He was called in for an interview and the personnel manager was impressed enough to arrange a second interview with the president of the company. It looked as if Franklin was going to get the job.

But then, when Franklin was at lunch with the personnel manager, he was asked his age. Fifty-two, he answered truthfully.

Franklin received a note two days later, saying the company had hired another applicant. He thought he had been discriminated against because of his age and filed a complaint.

He thought there would be a hearing within a week or two and the matter would be resolved. "No," said the clerk. "We'll be lucky if we get to it in the next two years."

"What do I do?" Franklin asked.

"Wait," the clerk answered, shrugging his shoulders.

There are a half-dozen major laws and a handful of presidential orders that ban discrimination in hiring on the basis or race, sex, age, religion, nationality, military service, or physical handicaps. But no agency enforces all these laws and each agency uses a different means of enforcement.

The victims of job bias are hurt the most by the bureaucratic tangle.

The Equal Employment Opportunity Commission is staggering under its huge case backlog. The cases represent pleas of workers who believe they have been denied jobs, promotions, or fair play because they are black, female, Spanish-speaking, or because they belong to unpopular religions.

Nearly 8,000 cases are filed each month, but fewer than 7,000 are resolved monthly.

It is up to the present administration to clear up this bureaucratic mess. We might as well not have the laws if we must wait two years to resolve a case.

Remember this: if you feel you're discriminated against, it may take two years to settle the case.

Let's get together to ask Congress to make the administration clear up this mess now.

The generalization in this speech—that it takes two years to resolve a bias complaint—is supported by statistical evidence and example. The writer follows the outline carefully, not mentioning all agencies concerned, feeling that a listing of the various agencies wouldn't enhance the speech's focus. His focus *is* the bureaucratic tangle.

Key words

Organize your speech around two or three key words that are easy to follow and remember. List these words and then expand on why each word was chosen. The words should emphasize the focus of the speech.

An example:

Confusion, uncertainty, and indifference are the major foes of the medical educator. For these three words sum up the challenges the educator faces in attempting to enlighten the public on preventative medicine.

The public, in a large part, is confused over claims and counter-claims on heart disease, cancer, even arthritis.

There are so many stories on the cause of heart disease—overeating, lack of exercise, smoking cigarettes—that the average man and woman is confused.

One group advocates a diet of no red meat or butter, while another group states red meat is fine but cut out bread and potatoes.

A third group advocates the elimination of salt and sugar in the daily diet as good preventative medicine.

Having read or heard all these stories, one asks a doctor for advice. He really can't give an answer. Why? Because these claims, even though they seem to make sense, haven't been thoroughly tested.

Confusion about cancer prevails among the public. This is equally true of arthritis, especially in the treatment of the disease.

The best advice for those of us with a touch of arthritis is to take aspirin and exercise moderately. This strategy is what several doctors recommend; others may tell you that heat is best.

Uncertainty is a real factor to deal with for the medical educator. There are those who believe that in many cases immunization is not necessary, that the medical profession has oversold the need for shots for many diseases.

These people do not belong to religious groups opposed to medical procedures. These men and women, many of them well-informed and well-read, are honestly uncertain about the need for so much immunization.

They question the need for a shot against smallpox, asking the date of the last reported case.

Indifference is a major foe. Indifference to good health practices undermines the country's total preventative program.

How can the medical profession win over the diseases that still plague us—heart problems, cancer, the neurological diseases—if the public's attitude is plain indifferent?

How many people still smoke cigarettes despite the warnings?

These three challenges—confusion, uncertainty and indifference —must be met head-on by medical educators.

All medical educators should strive to eradicate these three words.

And only through communication can we do so.

This speech, delivered to a recently graduated group of medical educators, employs three words as its basic structure. It shows that although most medical educators new in the field feel that indifference is their only challenge, confusion and uncertainty are problems, too.

Question and answer

The question-and-answer pattern follows a logical order, building on the speech's transitions to form the basic structure. Its goal is to draw the audience into immediate participation; the technique sets up the expectation of an answer. The method works well when the subject is technical in nature. For example, this speech was written for investors who were not extremely knowledgeable about the IRS code of taxable investments. Watch how the question-and-answer structure leads the audience step-by-step.

When a taxpayer sells an asset, a stock, a bond, a house, or a boat for more than he actually paid for it, he has what is termed a *capital gain*.

And when there is a capital gain, the Internal Revenue Service wants its share.

But what kind of share is equitable?

For more than a half a century, tax experts have wondered about that question. In fact, the present capital gains law is sort of an uneasy compromise that truly satisfies no one.

What is the present law?

In simple terms, the present law allows an individual to deduct sixty percent of a long-term gain from taxable income.

Hasn't the definition of *long-term gain* recently changed?

Yes—last year, a long-term gain was one made on property held for more than nine months. This year, the dividing line is up to a full year. Remember, too, a short-term gain is considered by the IRS as ordinary income, subject to full tax.

Well, that law isn't really so difficult or complicated, is it? It seems straight forward. No, the real problem is there are many other provisions. For example, there are special sections for home owners and there is a maximum rate on capital gains, rising as the taxpayer's income rises. Incidentally, corporations have a capital gains law all their own.

If capital gains, at least short term, are considered ordinary income by the IRS, aren't capital losses ordinary negative income?

If capital gains are fully included in taxable income in the year they're realized, capital losses should be fully subtracted from income in the year they are realized. Unfortunately, that's not the way the IRS sees it under the present law. They allow only a limited amount of income, two thousand dollars.

But isn't the administration saying it will change all that?

Well, they say in Washington that they are going to change it, but it's a safe bet that the administration does not plan to treat capital gains and losses in similar ways. The administration does not want a revenue loss and will propose to limit capital losses.

Isn't it true that preferential treatment of capital gains encourages investors to risk their funds in new, growing ventures?

Certainly. Preferential treatment of capital gains does increase the mobility of capital. It encourages it to move from stagnant or declining enterprises into businesses that offer better prospects for profit.

If all this is true, then, what is the problem, really?

Probably the biggest problem involved in dealing with capital gains is that they are realized by such diverse people in such diverse ways for such diverse reasons.

One person buys and sells stock regularly, hoping to make a profit by trading. Another person buys assets only for the income they yield.

It boils down to one thing: The government, with the long-term rule, is attempting to differentiate between these two individuals, the long-term investor and the short-term investor.

Notice that in this speech, the audience is aware of the transitions from one subject to the next. The speech may be short, but it covers extensive material with each section given the proper emphasis as the answer to a question.

Problem solving

The problem-solving structure in speech writing catches the audience's attention and interest. In this structure, you will state the problem, analyze it and suggest solutions, showing that your solution solves the problem. You then enlarge upon the solution by offering would-be solutions to the problem and eliminating those suggestions that would prove ineffective. Finally you will again bring up your solution as the speech's logical climax. Here's an example of a speech given to a suburban social club by an oil executive.

We have an energy crisis, obviously.

Every man, woman, and child in the United States is aware of this crisis—but our real challenge is increasing our energy supply.

The United States consumes energy at a far higher rate than it produces energy.

The stopgap measures to balance energy demand and supply not only fail to solve the problem but add to the uncertainty of the future.

The country must meet both short-term and long-term energy needs. In the immediate future, we will need energy to meet the requirements of a population estimated at two hundred forty-five million in less than thirteen years.

There are those who suggest that solar energy will solve the problem. But the problem with solar energy is that it does not meet an immediate need; it must be developed. How long this development process will take is difficult to estimate.

The flow of energy must be constant and assured. Oil and natural gas account for seventy-five percent of the nation's energy consumption. It will be the mainstay of supply at least for the forseeable future. These are the fuels, along with coal, which are of the most immediate concern.

The other part of the solution is the increased production and use of coal. Using coal means a stretch-out of the environmental timetables. The government must give a final decision on surface-mining rules to allow planning production accelerated.

Only with the program outlined can we hope to solve the immediate energy crisis.

This speech demonstrates how the solution of a problem can be worked into the speech's climax.

Start and finish

Openings

The opening and closing of a speech remain with an audience. They're vital to the success of the speech, and each part must stand on its own. Because your speech must flow from beginning to end, you will need to write a smooth transition from the opening into the main body of the speech and conclude the speech in a logical fashion.

In your introduction, try to capture the audience's attention, preparing them for your main point. Try some of these effective openings:

An anecdote:

When Roy and Mary Hiltz of Orange were looking for a new car two years ago, they had economy in mind. They used the official fuel economy ratings of the U.S. Environmental Protection Agency to make their decision. They wished they hadn't. These figures are a farce, Roy and Mary say, and they're angry.

A quotation:

"The government has falsified the fuel economy ratings of the new cars," consumer advocate John B. Brown states.

Mr. Brown says that an automobile manufacturer's survey shows that the average new car's gasoline mileage consumption is running twelve percent below the government's published figures.

A striking statement:

> When it comes to measuring fuel economy in new cars, even the federal government doesn't trust the federal government. The Department of Transportation discounts the Environmental Protection Agency estimates by eleven percent.

A structured statement:

> The gasoline mileage figures released by the U.S. Environmental Protection Agency aren't accurate. In fact, the agency readily admits these figures are just approximations and cannot be trusted.

A statement stressing the importance of the subject:

> If you purchase a new car and estimated your mileage costs for the year and then found you were paying one hundred fifty dollars more, you'd be upset.
> This is the lesson millions of car buyers are learning every year. And this is all due to false estimates by the U. S. Environmental Agency. Millions of Americans have been ripped off by inaccurate figures released by the federal government.

Closings

In the closing of your speech, leave the audience with a strong and lasting impression. Most speeches end by summarizing the major points or ideas presented. Although the practitioner may want to leave the audience gasping with inspiration from the rhetoric, this is not usually the case.

Strive for a natural conclusion. Many of the devices used in an opening of a speech are effective for the conclusion, such as an anecdote, quotation, striking statement, or structured statement. You could also conclude by stressing the importance of the subject. If a natural conclusion cannot be found to end the speech, give a summary of the speech.

Types of speeches

All speeches follow fundamental principles, but there are certain types that require specific writing techniques:

The report
Statement of position
Value

Policy
Entertainment
Special occasion

Report

A report speech can be boring, the speaker droning on with figures and
statistics until every member of the audience is praying for the speech to
end. But the report speech does not have to be a bore; with imagination
you can make it interesting and informative. The key is preparation.

When writing the speech, remember to begin and end firmly,
packaging the ideas for the audience. Give the material an interesting
focus; always look for new ways to present facts.

Carefully edit the material, leaving out those details that would lead
the audience away from your selected focus. Be concise; don't ramble on
and on. Here's an example of a report:

> Members of the Episcopal Church this year gave $275 million to the
> Church for all purposes. Of this amount, $13 million, or about five cents
> from each dollar, went to the Executive Council.
>
> What happened to the five pennies from your dollar? The Executive
> Council deals in services—services to people.
>
> Every program aims in one way or another to educate, to heal, to
> strengthen people.
>
> Wherever Council money goes, someone benefits: the aged, the
> handicapped, the drug addict, the alcoholic, the blind, the deaf, even
> the so-called "normal communicant."
>
> Not quite two and a half cents of your dollar went across the seas to
> provide missionary support. It aided more than sixteen hundred who
> worked as priests, evangelists, teachers, nurses, and social workers.
>
> The rest of the Executive Council nickel was used in continental
> United States, financing services too big, too general, or too technical
> for any one diocese to undertake itself.
>
> Examples range from the Church's ministry on college campuses to
> its work with Cuban refugees in Miami, from pilot projects in chang-
> ing urban communities to leadership training courses. It is likely that
> you, your family, or parish benefitted directly from one or more of
> these services.
>
> Any human problem is a religious problem. The Executive Council
> sponsored twelve "pilot dioceses" to explore contemporary urban life.
> How can the Church relate to the lives of people in blighted city
> neighborhoods? This is what these programs are attempting to discover.
>
> Education is one of the most important activities of the Council, yet it
> only takes three-tenths of a cent.

Some of the Church's most effective work in the struggle for human dignity is supported by three consultative services, church-sponsored birth control clinics, drug and alcoholic addiction clinics, and refugee sponsorship.

One cent was spent running the Church headquarters in New York and in public relations, the use of mass media to speak for the Church.

This then, in brief, is what the Executive Council does. One does what one can with five pennies.

Statement of position

Frequently you will want to write a statement of position speech telling how a company, institution, or organization stands on a topic. The goal of the speech is to give the company's side clearly and forcefully, being aware of the audience's sensitivity. The ideas should come across strong but respectful of the other side of the issue. As such, the tone is tactful, polite, and diplomatic without weakening the force of the company's argument.

You can review the position with questions such as these:

What do you believe?
What are the specific arguments for your view?
Are there points that must be conceded?
Do these concessions modify your side, or do your reasons lend themselves to a stronger, more convincing argument?

Think these objections through carefully until you're sure of each point. A point is struck out if it doesn't stand up. When you're sure, write the speech, being very careful not to sound arrogant or opinionated. Read this next example:

In 1974, Congress passed the Speedy Trial Act. The thought behind this legislation was to strengthen the Constitution's guarantee of a prompt trial for those accused of a federal crime by assuring swift trial and punishment.

Unfortunately, the law serves neither justice nor law enforcement. Complaints about this law come from all sides. Defense attorneys complain they don't have adequate time to prepare their defense.

Prosecutors say that the inflexible deadlines are forcing them to waste staff time, delay arrests and ignore some criminals they otherwise would be pursuing.

Judges say they can live with the deadlines, but it means long, weary hours on the bench, plus trial scheduling complexities. The act states that the time between arrest and indictment for a federal crime can't exceed thirty days; the time between the indictment and arraignment can't be more than ten days; and between arraignment and trial, sixty days.

One of the real problems: Cases that aren't tried on time must be dismissed. The law also authorized fines for attorneys who file frivolous motions or otherwise delay trial.

A major criticism of defense lawyers is that the timetable for speedy trials was designed mainly with street crimes in mind. The deadlines are far too short for many of the complicated cases, involving defendants charged with securities fraud, income tax invasion, and other white-collar crimes.

There is another problem attorneys have with the Speedy Trial Act. The attorneys argue that they usually are not called into a case until their client has been indicted by a Grand Jury. By that time prosecutors have a head start that in complicated cases could actually take years.

Legal observers generally are surprised by the negative impact of the law. Federal judges and the Justice Department representatives had argued that the deadlines were too inflexible. Defense attorneys, on the other hand, ignored the debate.

Congress passed the measure hastily, largely a tribute to Senator Sam Ervin, then retiring after 20 years in the Senate. The Watergate Committee Chairman stated that his goal was to cure a disgraceful situation. He said that justice was traveling on lead feet in the federal courts. There was no such thing as a speedy trial, he added.

Not everyone is critical of the act. There are some judges who think it is working great. Most of the judges, however, concede that "very complex" cases might cause problems.

We have tried the law in New York and it has not worked. The U.S. Attorney in New York complains that the short deadline problems outweigh the benefits.

The time prosecutors waste on extra trial preparations will eat into the time available for major investigations of Medicaid and securities fraud or big-time narcotics dealings.

Prosecutors are concerned that even if a delay is nobody's fault and the defendant has not been prejudiced, a case will have to be dismissed and the defendant will walk out free if deadlines aren't met.

The chief impact on judges has been to make their already hectic days even worse by complicating the scheduling of both civil and criminal trials. Some judges keep attorneys in several civil cases on the alert so these cases can be called up on short notice in case the defendant in a criminal trial pleads guilty.

We are not against swift trials and, overall, it is a desirable concept. But it is not working. It is not in the interests of the defendants, nor the prosecution, nor the judges on the bench.

Congress must change the law, allowing more time between arrest
and indictment, indictment and arraignment, and arraignment and trial.

This time, members of the bar must be heard by Congress on this
matter.

The value speech

The value speech praises an achievement or emphasizes the fundamental
ideals, such as peace, brotherhood, love of neighbor, or justice for all.
The subjects for a value speech are numerous.

Your challenge is to select the significant points and to present old,
time-worn ideas in fresh, impressive language.

Answer the following questions to help you steer the presentation of
your speech:

What is important about this event (person, achievement, project)?
How does it illustrate the values that we want to preserve?
How important are these values to us now?

As in other speech types, how the significant points are connected
depends on the degree of emphasis each point should receive. Appropriate style is important in a value speech, the language reflecting the
dignity of the subject. As such, humor must be restrained. The audience
becomes irritated if there is a hint of flippancy about a serious concern.

Use fairly formal language—slang should not be used—yet guard
against being pompous. Big words don't necessarily increase the dignity
of the speech and may make it sound artificial. At times there's a thin line
between artificial and formal.

It's better to understate the subject, give less praise, than to overstate
and blow the praise out of proportion. Trite phrases will defeat a speech's
effectiveness. Clichés are boring.

The major objective a writer hopes to achieve is for the audience to
say, "He deserves the praise," or "It's important to me," or "We need to
remember that." The speech's language must be precise if the audience is
to react this way. Concentrate on a specific word to carry the meaning;
the tone is built with details and full descriptive details are textured into
the delivery.

To be sure, emotionalism plays a role in the value speech. Some of
our deepest values are founded on emotions and an emotional appeal
can be used to great advantage. For example:

For those in mass communications, cynicism is a way of life. Most of
us are a bit jaded when it comes to knowing what a public figure is
really like.

Usually, the private image of the individual fails to match the public image. The public figure professes one side of an issue, yet in private life, he readily admits to his associates he is saying it only because it is a popular cause.

In the last decade, we have been associated with the Bishop. We have seen him lead the Diocese through an unprecedented period of upheaval and change.

Through this continuing, tense period, the Bishop has stood up courageously, doing what he believed was right.

He never failed to listen to both sides of a question. He always tried to see both sides of a question. He always tried to see the other point of view and then made his decision.

The Bishop recognized the many wrongs in our society and world. He spoke out against these wrongs publicly because he believed privately. He spoke on many issues long before it was popular to comment. He spoke out because he believed it was his duty to do so.

When the black community desperately attempted to have its voice heard by the school committee, the Bishop was the first religious leader to speak for their cause. When the students attended freedom schools for a day, he was there at the schools to show his tangible support.

The Bishop cares for people. This, in essence, is his greatness. He is a kind, gentle man, never seeking personal publicity. He seeks to help people make a better life.

Many of the church honestly couldn't understand why the Bishop would not stand aside and let things go on as before. As a sincere and dedicated Christian, he could not. As his career was ending as the Diocesan Bishop, he spoke against our antiquated abortion laws.

The Bishop did not have to speak publicly on this emotional issue. His days as an active religious leader were at a close.

Those very vocal forces on the other side of this controversial issue would vilify his name not only in the church but in public as well. This did not stop him. He is a man of personal integrity.

The Diocese is stronger because the Bishop has left his courage, honesty, and maturity as he dealt with the realities of contemporary life.

The policy speech

Although most speeches are persuasive, the policy speech's specific focus is persuasion, advocating the acceptance of a belief or suggesting a course of action.

In writing a policy speech, remember these two basic factors: the audience's level of comprehension and the length of the speech. Ask yourself, "Can the desired goal with this audience be accomplished? How much actual information will this audience need?" Other questions are "What does the audience know about the subject? What is their attitude?"

If the audience is sympathetic to your view, keep the tone low key. However, if the audience tends to be negative, write the speech with care, the thesis logically and tactfully presented. For an indifferent audience, prove the situation is serious and demand action. Emotional appeals, if used at all, must be used sparingly and with reason.

When writing, employ speech patterns suitable not only for the subject but for the audience as well. Present all arguments in a logical sequence.

No matter what the audience's attitude, a policy speech requires a strong introduction, winning the interest and sympathy of the audience. You should attempt to leave the audience with a memorable impression. The first kind of introduction, called *inductive*, opens with a striking statement to enlist immediate empathy. It then details all the facts and particulars of the subject. Use the inductive approach with a negative audience. On the other hand, a *deductive* introduction, employing deduction in reasoning, wins over an apathetic audience. In this method, you give them a solid reason why they should be interested.

Here are some ideas for writing a strong, persuasive speech:

1. Place the most telling argument at the conclusion, and the weakest argument in the middle.

2. Be diplomatic. Convey respect for the feelings and dignity of the audience. As you bring forth the thesis, use tact. A hostile audience will dismiss even the soundest argument if it lacks tact.

3. An analogy or a metaphor can be the foundation for the entire speech. Rhetorical questions may be used to good advantage; they force an internal answer from the audience.

4. Put a controversial point into a question instead of making a positive statement. This wins attention with the necessary tact.

The following example is a speech delivered to a mixed group of business leaders and journalists. The purpose of the meeting was to discuss business and industrial news coverage, but the business leaders far outnumbered the news persons. Both were wary of each other to a point. Notice that this speech gives both sides equal credit and suggests a course of action.

> People in business and industry find the press lacking. Any time a group of executives gather, the conversation usually focuses on what is wrong with the news media.

There are two major gripes against the press from our business, financial, and industrial leaders. First, they say, the press is prejudiced, out to get business.

Second, the reporting of economic news is incompetent; the average business reporter lacks a fundamental knowledge of the workings of most of America's largest corporations.

Members of the business press, on the other hand, have a gripe or two about business and the problems of covering it. First, the writers say, business leaders have a habit of writing news releases without any real news in the stories. And when a reporter tries to dig up additional information, the door is closed quite firmly.

In fact, most journalists add if they employed the aggressive tactics of their fellow political reporters, there would be a loud howl from every corporate manager in the country.

Business leaders argue that the real problem is that most reporters aren't knowledgeable about business and finance.

Corporations, in fact, have in the past few years underwritten business and economic fellowships for journalists. These corporations hope that by returning to the college campus, reporters will understand the corporations' problems and will upgrade the business sections in the nation's press.

On the surface, certainly, this is a healthy approach to the problem; or is it? Is there a conflict of interest? Would not the sponsoring companies expect favorable press treatment?

Is the journalist compromising his or her integrity by being paid to go back to school by a company?

No, answers John P. Drake, president of one of America's giant insurance companies. He says that the relationship between the press and business is like two strange dogs circling each other warily, suspicious of each other's intentions. The education programs, he maintains, will result in better understanding between the two. And that is businesses' goal in these fellowships: better understanding.

Most business leaders would agree. They expect nothing from these educational ventures other than the hope of dealing with more sophisticated reporters in the future.

Academics at institutions offering these fellowships for journalists say these programs are certainly needed. They point to the fact that reporters covering other news beats (the courts, the state house, the federal regulatory boards) usually have a solid knowledge of their subject. Business writers do not.

Many journalists who received these fellowships say that they were unaware the courses offered were being paid for by corporations. The fellowship literature published by the schools does not list the sponsors. It is not until the students report to school that sponsors are revealed. Some of the reporters say that they feel compromised.

The fact is, of course, no matter who sponsors these fellowships, there is a need for them. Business reporting must have perspective and sophistication. Business deserves understanding and accuracy in its news coverage.

These fellowships are already set up by business and industry. Could not the news media, newspapers, magazines, radio, and television —most of them giant corporations in their own right—combine with the business and industrial leaders in a joint effort to underwrite a comprehensive educational program for business writers and reporters?

Professional men and women—doctors, lawyers, educators—return to the classroom for further study during their careers.

The business reporters should have the same opportunity, but without the fear of conflict of interest.

When the members of the news media join in the venture with a financial commitment, the problem will be solved and we can look forward to an enlightened business press.

Entertainment

Occasionally you'll receive a request to write a "light" speech, merely for entertainment. It's a sticky assignment, even though there's usually no research involved. The speech must be tight, the story well told.

However, there are guidelines you can follow. Usually you're writing it for one of the top executives or managers of the company or organization. The first rule is to know how well the executive speaks; is he an accomplished speaker, articulate, able to hold an audience? Or is the speaker less than an orator? You'll want to write the speech accordingly.

Inexperienced writers try too hard in putting the speech together. These writers tend to make up for the lack of a defined subject with rhetoric. They ramble from point to point.

A "light" speech doesn't necessarily mean that the audience has to fall in the aisles with laughter. Don't work too hard to be overly funny, because forced humor will leave the audience flat. Remember that the ability to write humor is a special talent that few otherwise competent writers possess. Instead, think about being *entertaining*; include incidents or stories because they are unique or enlivening. When writing, share an adventure with the audience. Build the story to a climax or surprise ending, structuring details into the speech, preparing the audience for the outcome without giving it away. The story told in the speech should make a point, the point fitting the purpose of the speech.

Pay particular attention to the ending. A good ending leaves the audience with a pleasant feeling; and this is the goal of an entertainment speech, a pleasant feeling. Even if the speaker leaves much to be desired, the speech will be a success if the audience leaves in a pleasant mood.

Here's an example of an entertainment speech:

No matter what the club announcement says on the bulletin board, there is no such thing in the game of tennis as a nice, friendly tournament.

Every Labor Day weekend, the bulletin board announces the annual club tournament. And despite the disappointments and traumas of years gone by, every one signs up. This year, vow all the losers, it is going to be different.

So why do we play?

Some players claim, with due modesty, to help the club out, to insure sufficient entries. Others secretly fantasize that they are going to win the tournament this Labor Day.

They never do.

In club tourneys, the finalists are as predictable as the next high tide, unless they are felled by flying rackets in the opening rounds. This gambit is not unknown, incidentally, where rivalries run deep.

Troubles really start before the first round of the tournament is ever played.

Can the male member of a husband and wife team in the mixed doubles competition dump his spouse for a younger gal with terrific ground strokes and an equally terrific figure? Or in this day of liberation, can the wife dump her husband for some fleet-footed, great-serving youth?

Or supposing you elect to stay with your spouse and bravely play the tournament. She missed an easy shot and you say, "watch it." She gives you one of those looks that melt icebergs.

Your neighbor, Harry, who was the top player on his college team, enters the intermediate group. Why isn't he playing the advanced? He asks you the same question. And sure enough he beats you in the first round on Saturday morning. See if I let him borrow my ladder again.

Frank and Bob win the men's doubles, as usual. Marion and Bill win the mixed doubles as usual. And John wins the advanced men's singles, as usual.

I didn't get out of the first round, as usual. Well, what the hell, we do it for fun, don't we? Isn't that what it is all about, fun?

Anyway, if I work on my backhand and take some lessons on my serve this winter, who knows?

I still could win next Labor Day.

Special occasion

The special occasion speech covers a multiplicity of events. It includes the introduction of a guest or speaker, the presentation or acceptance of an award, a farewell, the dedication of a memorial, or an expression of goodwill.

Introduction of a guest or speaker. The introduction of a guest or speaker calls for research. Select details of the speaker's career or life that best describe the highlights. Keep the introduction brief. For example:

> Our guest speaker tonight is a man whose name is known to literally thousands of newspaper readers. His byline and column are carried by more than twenty of the largest mass circulation newspapers in this country and Canada.
>
> He started his newspaper career in Boston as a City Hall reporter for the old Boston Transcript. He then went to the New York Herald Tribune as the Washington correspondent for that famed newspaper.
>
> He won three Associated Press awards for excellence in reporting during the Eisenhower and Kennedy administrations, and in 1964, he signed a contract with the Scripts Howard syndicate to write a column out of Washington about Washington.
>
> He enjoys the confidence of many high in our government and has broken a number of important stories.
>
> His story on President Nixon's first trip to China when it still was in the planning stages was his most important exclusive. He has authored several books on national and international politics.
>
> Our speaker, John G. Ellis.

Presentation. A presentation speech is usually a bit longer than an introduction, characteristically praising the recipient of the award. List their accomplishments and explain the purpose of the award. For example:

> When Robert Jordan passed away a decade ago, his colleagues, associates, and friends felt there should be a fitting memorial to his work and life.
>
> He was an attorney who believed in the simple truths: honesty, courage, and above all, justice. Thus, the Robert Jordan Memorial Award was born. It is annually awarded to an attorney in this community who best exemplifies the professional and private life of Robert Jordan.

The recipient of the Robert Jordan Memorial Award this year certainly emulates the best of the Jordan tradition. A graduate of Middlesex Law School at age twenty-four, he passed the bar two weeks after graduation. Instead of trying to find a position with a law firm, he opened his own law office in our community.

His office is always open for those in trouble or need. No case is too small for him to try. No one is ever turned away because they could not pay a fee.

For more than a quarter of a century this man, quietly and with dignity, has fought for the deprived; has fought for those in need; has fought for those when others turned their backs.

He has won a great many cases by his honest belief in justice for all.

Ladies and gentlemen, this year's Robert Jordan Memorial Award winner, Attorney Rubin K. Solomon.

Acceptance. Acceptance speeches are usually short, a gracious response to the presentation. Humility is always observed. Here's an example:

Thank you for this award. I knew Robert Jordan and I admired him, not only for his ability as a lawyer, but as a man, a humanitarian.

To think that I, in some small way, practice law in the Robert Jordan tradition leaves me feeling very humble, indeed.

This award will be placed on my wall in my office so each day I can look at it and hope that I may be more like Robert Jordan.

For if I can accomplish only a quarter in my lifetime what Robert Jordan did in his, I will have lived a full life.

Farewell. Farewell speeches are vocal tributes, stressing the significant achievements of the honored person. You'll need to also lighten the speech, here and there, with nonserious incidents or comments.

You do not need to write too much sentimentality into the speech. If the tribute tends to be too flowery, the effectiveness of a sincere tribute can be reduced.

An example:

Percy J. Lynch is retiring tonight after a half of century of being a working journalist.

Mr. Lynch has probably worked more news stories than any other journalist in this city. His first byline with the old Boston Post was the story of the armistice in World War I. He probably saw more life in the roaring twenties than any television script writer could imagine.

His story of Lindberg's flight across the Atlantic is still being quoted by journalism teachers. His story on the veterans' march on Washington was nominated for a Pulitzer prize.

Even though Mr. Lynch was not as active on the street beat as he was in his younger days, he never lost that zest for a good story and a well-written lead.

My favorite of his stories is not a world-shattering news report. It is a simple story and has a simple lead. At the time he was covering evangelist Billy Graham and wanted to interview him, but couldn't get to see Mr. Graham.

His lead next morning was "I coudn't see Billy Graham last night to save my soul."

We say farewell to Percy J. Lynch tonight after fifty years of service to American journalism. His work and mark will live forever.

Memorials. Memorials are serious in tone, smooth in style, and well integrated.

Today we dedicate this memorial in the memory of a woman who will always live in our thoughts.

Marion Lyons was a nurse in the best tradition of that profession. Her patience, her understanding, and her genuine love for life inspired her fellow workers and comforted countless patients.

Our hospital is a far better institution today because Marion Lyons served on our nursing staff for twenty years.

It is only fitting that this plaque be permanently placed in our front lobby for all to see and remember her by.

Goodwill. A simple expression of goodwill can be generous and touching. Its intentions are

We like you.
We all want the same things.
We are friends.

Honesty is important in goodwill speeches, so the points made must be genuine. An artificial approach turns off an audience. Make sure that you show respect for the audience as in this speech:

I am here today to bring greetings to faculty from the Board of Trustees. All too often faculty and administration distrust trustees, feeling that they're not sympathetic to problems and challenges.

I speak for my fellow board members when I say we are sympathetic; we do understand the many problems and challenges you face each day. We know of your work, even the personal sacrifices you make for the good of the school. We know of the intense loyalty you have for this school.

If these statements were not true, the turnover in faculty and administration would be far greater than it is. A great majority have been at the school for more than a decade.

We share your concerns. We share your goals. Our responsibility as members of the Board of Trustees is to help you to reach these goals. Together we can reach these goals; we can meet these challenges, as a team.

Summary

The practitioner knows a speech requires two steps before it is written. First, the subject and the approach are considered. Second, the audience is considered, their beliefs and knowledge. The writer then integrates approach and audience to present an effective speech. Remember that the examples in this chapter were written for specific occasions and should not be used as an outline for a speech for a similar event; write in your own style.

7

Visuals

A visual presentation tells an organization's story dramatically. With the right balance between imagination and taste, it can be extremely effective. That's why such presentations are being employed more and more by practitioners, especially those working for large corporations or organizations with country-wide publics.

When designing a visual presentation, first ask yourself "Who is the audience? What does the audience know about the subject?" Or if those questions are not pertinent, "What does the audience believe, and why?" Obviously the reason for asking such questions about the audience is that their knowledge matches the degree of sophistication of your presentation. Their background and beliefs dictate the presentation's pace. For example, one practitioner envisioned a multimedia presentation including film, slides, and sound, all tied into a fast-moving, highly charged half-hour designed to influence by shock. Technically the presentation could have won an award, but it was so fast moving that the audience got lost. They didn't know as much about the subject as the practitioner assumed they did. Naturally some individual members of the audience were delighted, entertained, and impressed by the display. But the basic public relations goal, that of influencing the audience, was not met. The audience couldn't understand the company's viewpoint and thus couldn't decide whether it was a correct viewpoint or not. Especially if the presentation is to be shown to a number of audiences, there must be a balance, allowing those with little or no knowledge to understand the message along with those with an advanced knowledge. This is not to say that the presentation should be so basic as to be boring.

Remember, too, that whereas a speech may be rewritten to meet each audience's level of knowledge, a film, once shot, edited, and recorded is more or less permanent. It is difficult and costly to redo a sound track or reshoot a scene to be incorporated into an already edited film. Slides, on the other hand, are more flexible. A slide show can always be updated with new slides and script.

There are several factors in determining the type of visual presentation. Budget, of course, is important, but it isn't the only factor in the decision. Subject plays an important role. For example, for one story film might be the most effective vehicle, but a slide presentation might be more desirable for another subject. So, if costs are equal, you should decide which of the two media, film or slides, is best suited for your subject. Although the prospect of shooting a film is exciting, a down-to-earth determination is necessary.

After choosing the medium, you'll determine the length. There are no guidelines on how long a presentation should be, but most experienced communicators agree that one-half hour or less is the maximum length for a documentary film. A well-edited film should make its point in this amount of time, including the introduction and credits. The average slide presentation should take between fifteen and twenty minutes.

Some inexperienced practitioners try to "beat the budget" by shooting the film or slides themselves or having a "talented amateur" do it. The results are usually disastrous; the audience becomes bored with home movies every time. In contrast, professionals, given a decent script, can make the presentation effective, smooth, and interesting to the audience.

Film

Working script

Your initial assignment in film is to write a rough script, describing the action, scenes, and narration. You must be sure of the script's accuracy.

If the film is about a subject you're familiar with, you won't have too much difficulty. But if your knowledge is sparse, you must research the subject well. Make sure you have a comprehensive knowledge of the subject before starting the script.

A working script should outline the content of the film. It gives the person in charge of production (the photographer or director) an idea of what to shoot and the basic, overall premise of the film.

After you discuss the technical aspects of the script with the production people and you review the story line with management, you can write a shooting script. This script is a revision, giving the director/photographer full details and instructions for the film from the first scene to conclusion.

Some production houses take the shooting script and do a storyboard on each scene to be shot. The storyboard shows the action with stick figures, Polaroid photographs, or even full drawings with pastels or felt-tip pens. The art is placed in a box above the narration or dialogue. Whether a storyboard is used is up to the production people. Most directors/photographers work with simply a shooting script, rather than a storyboard.

Most public relations films are documentary, journalistic in nature; they report the facts. Some films use a "voice-over" technique, in which a narrator offscreen describes the action. In this method, you shoot the scenes first, without sound, and then record the "voice over" in a studio. It is less expensive this way than shooting sound (dialogue) on location.

However, as filmmaking grows in stature not only as a communication medium but as an effective public relations technique, many cinematographers prefer *cinema verité,* natural sound, candid realism. Filmmakers want the film to appear as if the cameras, lights, sound equipment, and crew weren't there at all. This look isn't easy. Most of the people in documentaries are not actors and the experience is unique to them. Some will be conscious of the filming and their voices and movements will be less than natural. Some filmmakers minimize this problem by shooting with an empty camera for several minutes. When the participants become accustomed to the cameras and lights, they are less inhibited.

Preparation before shooting a scene takes time. Because lighting is critical, it may take several hours. A good cinematographer takes time to make sure it is correct.

If sound is being recorded while the scene is being filmed, it is important to get clear, intelligible dialogue recorded in synchronization with the lip motions of those speaking. Microphones must be close to the speakers. The sound track should have "presence," meaning that the speakers' voices should sound near the listener. Placing mikes near the speakers will also minimize unwanted background noises. There are a number of excellent techniques to achieve "presence," including the use of lapel or pistol microphones. Remember that sometimes, for the sake of authenticity, background noises are desirable. The director will help you decide when background is needed.

Let's examine production on a film about how a bank functions within a community. Sue Kahl, a public relations practitioner for a state banking association, wrote the script at the request of the member banks of the association. Their research had shown a lack of understanding among the general public on the many functions of a bank.

Sue decided to follow a business day at the bank from start to finish, giving the film a logical opening and conclusion. Within this format, Sue could present the bank's functions visually. She wanted to use a mixture of "voice over" and dialogue.

First she located a typical community bank to use as a set. She planned to shoot the film when the bank was not open for business (afterhours and on weekends).

Note that in the working script, Sue did not make extensive camera suggestions. As the film is being shot, the cinematographer works out the camera angles.

Here's her working script:

Scene One

LONG SHOT OF BANK'S SIGN

PAN TO FRONT DOOR

CLOSE-UP OF CLOCK TO ESTABLISH TIME, 8 A.M.

GUARD OPENS DOOR TO ALLOW EMPLOYEES IN THE BANK

SEVEN OR EIGHT EMPLOYEES ENTER THE BANK

Narrator:

The town of Plainville is starting its business day. The staff of the Plainville National Bank is reporting to work. The guard, Jim, lets the employees in. Here's the president, John Roche.

SHOT OF INSIDE THE BANK

TELLERS COUNTING OUT MONEY

OFFICERS AT THEIR DESKS

THE TELLER AT THE "WALK-UP WINDOW" IS BUSY CASHING CHECKS

Narrator:

Even though the bank does not open for another hour, it is still busy. (*Noises from the floor, walk-up window, etc.*)

Scene Two

CLOSE-UP OF CLOCK, 9 A.M.

GUARD OPENS DOOR

BANK FILLS WITH CUSTOMERS

SHOTS OF TELLERS WITH CUSTOMERS

Narrator:

The day starts: cashing checks, taking deposits. And all this is tied into a computer. Did you ever consider what it would be like without a bank in your community?

CLOSE-UP OF BOB BROWN, LOAN OFFICER

HE SHAKES HANDS WITH CUSTOMER

CLOSE-UP OF BROWN AND CUSTOMER

Bob Brown:

Well, Harry, how are you?

Harry:

Fine, Bob, the store is doing well, but I need some help. Have to buy for Christmas, you know. Need about twenty thousand for holiday merchandise.

Bob Brown:

Harry, I can't see any problem. Let me check the records and I'll propose it to the board this afternoon. We have your latest financial statements?

Harry:

Yes, you have the latest.

Narrator:

This is one of the functions of the commercial bank, loaning funds to business people. Bob Brown is a loan officer and it is his responsibility to make sure Harry is able to pay back the loan.

SHOT OF BOOKKEEPING DEPARTMENT
LONG SHOT OF MACHINES WORKING

Narrator:

The bookkeeping department plays a vital role in the bank. Deposits are recorded, checks paid; all the financial data is recorded here. Thousands of accounts—business, government, private—are recorded with the aid of computers.

LONG SHOT OF SAFE DEPOSIT DEPARTMENT
CUT TO BARRED DOOR WITH ATTENDANT
CUSTOMER ENTERS AND OPENS SAFE DEPOSIT BOX

Narrator:

Customers rent safe deposit boxes to keep valuable papers, even jewelry, from being stolen or lost.

LONG SHOT OF OFFICERS AT DESK IN BANK LOBBY
CLOSE-UP OF FRANK HARRIS, TRUST OFFICER
HE GREETS AN ELDERLY WOMAN

Narrator:

This is Frank Harris, a trust officer. He manages funds for organizations and individuals as a fiduciary. He is greeting Martha Burnham, a widow, who lives on the proceeds of a trust fund.

CLOSE-UP OF JACK KING, COLLEGE STUDENT
HAPPY EXPRESSION ON JACK'S FACE AS HE TALKS TO HARRIS

Narrator:

Jack King, college student, receives a monthly check from a trust fund set up in his late parents' will. Mr. Harris watches over the young man's funds, according to the terms of the trust fund.

Scene Three

LONG SHOT OF BOARD OF DIRECTORS MEETING, WITH BANK
  PRESIDENT AT HEAD OF TABLE, PRESIDING
VARIOUS CLOSE-UP SHOTS OF DIRECTORS DURING MEETING

Narrator:

This is the weekly meeting of the Board of Directors. They are responsible for the overall operation of the bank and supervise the officers. Major decisions are voted on by the Board, the members being business and professional people of the community. There are two attorneys, a physician, the president of an electronic company, an insurance executive, a store owner, an architect, a textile mill president, a newspaper publisher, and the president and executive vice-president of the bank.

Scene Four

PAN LOBBY
SHOTS OF OFFICERS AND TELLERS WORKING

Narrator

The bank is closed, but the tellers must balance the books. All departments are working even though the front door is locked. This is just one day at a bank. But think for a moment—without a bank, the community would have a difficult time in doing business. This is what a bank is all about—a service to the community.

When Sue presented the working script to the officers of the banking association, they felt that it did not reflect a modern bank in a growing community. So she made several major revisions, focusing on community growth and the bank's role. She eliminated the dialogue between the merchant and the loan officer.

Other objections to the working script included a feeling that the narration was stilted in parts, that the script needed to be more dramatic, with more action and bank shots, using less narration.

It's good to remember that the number of pages of a shooting script is ten to fifteen per half-hour of film. Most writers tend to write too much narration. Because the visual side dominates, the narration should be "tight." Appropriate music usually is put in the background; your narrator does not have to talk constantly.

Shooting script

This is the shooting script Sue came up with:

Scene One

TRAFFIC SHOTS OF MAIN STREET, PLAINVILLE
LOTS OF ACTION—PEOPLE IN AND OUT OF STORES, TRAFFIC,
   AUTOMOBILES
CREATE A SENSE OF VITALITY
IMPRESSION OF PROGRESSIVE TOWN

Narrator:

This is Plainville. And these are the residents, working and shopping. It is a rapidly growing town with new businesses, homes, and stores. And, yet, the town has been here for a while—a century.

Scene Two

SHOTS OF THE TOWN: PLAINVILLE'S COLLEGE CAMPUS, PLAINVILLE
   POST, CHURCHES, MAIN OFFICE OF PLAINVILLE NATIONAL BANK,
   FIVE BANK BRANCHES

Narrator:

A number of Plainville businesses and institutions are a hundred years old. Plainville College, with two thousand undergraduates, is one hundred and forty-one years old. The Plainville *Post* is nearly a hundred and fifty years old and was founded the same year as the Plainville National Bank.

Scene Three

SHOTS OF NEW HOUSING CONSTRUCTION
YOUNG FAMILIES MOVING IN
SHOTS OF NEW PLANTS, ELECTRONIC FIRMS, EXTERIOR AND
   INTERIOR

Narrator:

And Plainville is growing: five new plants within a four-year period, fifteen hundred new jobs. The administration and the Chamber of Commerce have worked hard to bring in new industry.

SHOT OF CONSTRUCTION OF A PLANT, STEEL BEING ERECTED

Narrator:

The Plainville National Bank helped the town grow. The bank aided these companies in financing their new plants. The bank loaned directly to two of the companies and assisted in the financing of others. With fifteen hundred new jobs, at least a thousand families moved into town. New homes were built, the bank financing a great many of these—loaning funds to contracts and granting mortgages to the new families.

SHOT OF AUTOMOBILE DEALERSHIP, NEW CARS
NEW SUPERMARKET, PEOPLE SHOPPING
SHOW A LOT OF VITALITY

Narrator

And when the town grows and the population increases, businesses expand and stores are built to meet the new needs. And the bank helps these businesses and stores in financing their expansion programs.

Scene Four

INTERIOR SHOTS OF PLAINVILLE NATIONAL BANK
ZOOM-IN ON OFFICERS TALKING TO CUSTOMERS
ONE OFFICER IS OPENING A NEW CHECKING ACCOUNT
ANOTHER TAKES AN APPLICATION FOR A CAR LOAN

Narrator:

A bank provides many needed services: personal checking accounts, loans for new automobiles.

CAMERA TAKES LONG SHOT OF LOBBY
ZOOM-IN ON FRANK HARRIS, TRUST OFFICER
HE GREETS WOMAN

Narrator:

Frank Harris is a fiduciary. He manages trust funds. He is greeting Martha Burnham, a widow, whose trust fund he manages.

CLOSE-UP OF JACK KING, COLLEGE STUDENT, TALKING TO HARRIS

Narrator:

Jack King, college student, receives a monthly payment from a trust fund set up in his late parents' will. Mr. Harris watches over Jack's funds in a trust.

Scene Five

LONG SHOT OF BOARD OF DIRECTORS MEETING
THE PRESIDENT, JOHN ROCHE, PRESIDES

VARIOUS CLOSE-UP OF DIRECTORS SITTING AT TABLE AS MEETING
PROGRESSES

Narrator:

The Board of Directors of the bank meet weekly. They are responsible for the
bank's overall operation. The daily operation is conducted by the officers, with
John Roche, the president. Major decisions are the responsibility of the Board.
The directors are business and professional people, two attorneys, a physician, an
electronic company president, an insurance executive, a store owner, an
architect, a newspaper publisher, and the president and executive vice-president
of the bank.

Scene Six

JOHN ROCHE AT HIS DESK—MEDIUM SHOT AND THEN ZOOM IN
HE SPEAKS DIRECTLY TO CAMERA

Roche:

A community bank plays a unique role. We provide services to our customers, so
they, in turn, may grow. The bank must be innovative, progressive. We meet the
needs of our customers. Several of our town's plants ship overseas and we
provide letters of credit. We finance new industries as well as those well-
established in our community. One of our largest departments is our consumer
division, where we provide all types of personal banking services, from checking
and savings accounts to loans for all purposes—automobiles, dental, medical,
furniture, tuition. Your bank is here to serve you.

Editing and sound timetable

Sue really must think about a timetable when producing the film. For this
film, shot on location afterhours and on weekends, two or three weeks
shooting time is not unrealistic.

After shooting, the production people make a rough cut or a work
print. They put into sequence the six scenes. The film is edited from
the work print, with parts of scenes eliminated, and various camera angles used instead of others for the proper overall visual effect.

In rare instances a scene is reshot or substituted for another scene.
To avoid having to do this, a good cinematographer films a scene several times until he is sure he's got what he wants.

For cost reasons, most sound for this film is added after the film is
completed, using the voice-over technique. The narrator records the

script; his words are timed to the scenes being shown on the screen. However, the bank president's speech was done on film.

Editing and putting in the sound takes a minimum of six to eight weeks. The whole production from start until it is ready to be shown to an audience takes four or five months.

Slides

Slides can illustrate a point, fit a specific fact and effectively influence an audience. You will find slide presentations a versatile tool for many reasons involving subject, audience, and budget. First, a presentation can include diagrams and charts or actual scenes; it is flexible to your subject. Second, you can add or delete slides and narrative to tailor your program to a specific group. Third, because a "live" speaker can control the slide movement in and out of the projector with a remote control switch, you can pace the flow to different audiences. If the speaker does not want to operate the slides, another person can be at the projector to switch frames.

Pace

Unlike a film, a slide presentation must correlate *exactly* with the narrative. In a film the voice-over announcer on the sound track might be still describing a subject as the scene fades without any undue harm to the overall effectiveness of the presentation. But in a slide program, if one slide is on the screen while the speaker describes another subject, it is terribly disconcerting to the audience.

Some narrations can be recorded so that the sound track has an automatic pulse to trip the slide from the magazine into the projector. There are even some projectors that will dissolve the picture on the screen before the next slide is shown.

Visual pace is important. The presentation must move, but don't go so fast that the audience loses the content. If slides are flashed too rapidly, the message loses impact.

There's disagreement about how many words should be spoken per slide. Some advocate using as many words as needed. But most experienced producers of slide presentations feel that a slide should be shown less than ten seconds, preferably five to seven seconds. Using this rule, two words spoken per second, a guide of ten to fourteen words per slide seems adequate. Thus a fifteen-minute presentation would require approximately 120–180 slides and 900–2,500 words of narration. As said before, the slide dominates the presentation and the narrator does not have to continually speak. Make sure you time the presentation before it is given.

Production

Simplicity is the key to the content of a slide, especially when creating charts and diagrams. If the chart or diagram is complicated with too many lines or colors, the message will be confusing.

When preparing art to be photographed, do not use black letters or figures on a dark background, or white letters on a light background. Although these combinations may look all right in art form, they do not photograph well, especially when photographed in black and white.

Instead of using one complex chart or diagram, show two or three charts or diagrams. The audience will be better able to absorb an idea presented in sequence rather than in one long, complicated visual.

As a general rule, regular 2″ × 2″ slides work best because they fit into the regular, home-type projectors, and they are easier to make and less expensive than other sizes.

The following is an example of a slide presentation. It's called "Common Sense about Weight Loss for Women" and was shown to women's clubs and organizations as a public service by a company sponsoring health-related clinics. On the left is the suggested visual to match the narration on the right.

Slide	*Narration*
Cartoon of fat woman with question mark.	Most of us are confused about weight loss.
Eagle in gym shorts with jogging shoes.	The federal government preaches holding to a safe weight level.
Montage of newspapers, magazines, radios, television sets.	What is confusing is the announcements of "sensational" new diets.
Cartoon of woman with a questioning expression.	Common sense tells us not to believe wild claims.

Slide	*Narration*
Cartoon of woman, head in clouds.	We want to believe there is an easy, simple way.
Type: The American Society of Bariatics; montage of ads for fad diets.	The American Society of Bariatics warns that there are more people on fad diets than on sound ones.
Type over visual of crowd: 70 million Americans.	More than seventy million Americans are overweight.
Cartoon of woman with bicycle puffing up huge hill.	There is no short cut to controlling weight.
Cartoon of woman with tape over her mouth.	What is common sense about weight loss for women?
Type: Diet or exercise?	What is the most beneficial: diet or exercise?
Cartoon of doctors in debate.	Each side, diet or exercise, has respected advocates.
Chart listing two types of exercise, two types of food, and calories gained and expended.	If you reduce your caloric intake below the amount your body expends, you lose weight.
Cartoon of stored calories.	Fat, or stored calories, causes weight.
Photo of diet book.	If you lose weight by dieting—why don't you diet?
Cartoon of woman lounging in front of TV.	Experts agree, but there is a problem. If you don't exercise, flab will remain.
Cartoon of woman looking in mirror, jar of wrinkle remover on table.	Many mature women lose weight and age overnight.
Close-up of woman's wrinkled neck.	This is a chicken neck after weight loss.

Slides	Narration
Photograph of woman exercising with someone giving her direction.	By exercising correctly, under professional supervision, this will not happen.
Cartoon of woman at table with heaps of food.	Does regular exercise cause you to eat more? Nonsense.
Photograph of person taking down data while observing college kid bench press.	A study by a university termed this a myth.
Photograph of report pages with quote in colored type over photo.	The report states, "Exercise does not increase appetite."
Photographs of a report diagram.	There is a difference between physical labor and exercise.
Split frame—left, photo of men digging ditch; right, women exercising.	Physical labor means eight hours of work, while exercise is one or two.
Split frame—left, chart showing calorie count; right, showing calisthenics.	A sensible diet with an exercise program is successful in weight loss.
Cartoon of women exercising.	Some feel only exercise is needed to lose weight.
Cartoon of woman looking happy and pleased.	You certainly will feel better.
Cartoon of unhappy woman.	But the lost weight will be minimal—water loss more than fat loss.
Action photograph of woman golfers.	Exercise is marvelous. Congratulations to those who play 18 every day.
Action photograph of women tennis players.	Or two sets of tennis.

Video	Narration
Chart of life expectancy.	Being overweight reduces your life expectancy.
Anatomy of a human body.	The human body, complex and complicated, functions with ease.
Muscle chart of body.	Muscles are the motors of your body.
Muscle chart of body section.	Each muscle has a singular function.
Type: Exercise	Rehabilitation (physical medicine) stresses exercise therapy.
Photograph of physical therapy department with therapists and patients.	Stroke victims or those with other physical disabilities exercise to recover.
Another photograph of rehabilitation unit.	Doctors know that a muscle not used because of injury will stop functioning.
Photo of woman pointing to date calendar marked on Tuesday "3 P.M., Tennis."	It is important to exercise regularly.
Cartoon of exhausted woman.	Exercise must be done within reason.

Slides	*Narration*
Photograph of exercise group with leader. Adult ballet class.	Exercise, controlled and regulated under professional supervision, is best.
Type: Exercise Diet Behavior modification	Exercise and diet, with behavior modification, is the answer.
Montage of diets, exercise charts.	The question: What type of diet and exercise?
Photograph of woman having medical examination. Cartoon of three women, each of very different looks.	Consult a physician before you undergo any dramatic weight loss. Each person is an individual.
Type: Guidelines	These are guidelines that have been successful.
Cartoon of woman pushing away food.	Dieting does not mean to stop eating entirely.
Photograph chart of four food groups.	A good diet is a safe one, nutritionally balanced.
Photo of plate of food counting up to 500 calories.	A 500 calorie maximum per day diet is not safe.
Montage of ads for fad diets.	Most "miracle" diets, advertised indiscriminately, are dangerous.
Type and drawing: Liquid protein diet within circle with line through it.	The federal government warns against the liquid protein diet.
A newspaper headline photo.	A dozen deaths have been attributed to the liquid protein diet.
Type frame listing three chronic diseases.	The diet is dangerous for those suffering from a chronic disease.
Cartoon of bald woman.	Many people have annoying symptoms from this diet even if they are well.

to be eaten

Cartoon of woman
on scale, very
happy

Cartoon of same
woman on scale
not happy

The less carbohydrates,
the less energy. The more
carbohydrates, such...

...there is an immediate
weight loss

The weight loss is
water, and fat... the
weight is regained.

Chart of how body
burns fat.

The body burns fats for fuel
when there are no carbohydrates.

Second chart.

There is a sharp rise of compounds
called keystones in the blood and
urine.

Third chart.

Nausea, vomiting, fatigue, apathy,
and low blood pressure results.

Type: Macrobotic
diet

The Macrobotic diet is
reasonably well balanced but not
without danger.

Photo of woman
eating rice.

Those who progress to the
higher level risk malnutrition. The
dieter subsists solely on rice.

Chart showing needed
proteins, vitamins,
and minerals.

With a lack of proteins,
vitamins and minerals, the
dieter starves nutritionally.

Cartoon of woman
fasting.

Fasting is dangerous. It
robs the body of essential nutrients.

Photo of pills.

One of the greatest hazards are the
weight-reduction pills.

Type:
Amphetamines

Amphetamines at times
are prescribed to get the dieter
started.

Woman reaching for pills
in bathroom medicine
cabinet.

They become ineffective
and continued use can
cause addiction.

Photo over-the-shoulder
of woman writing on
legal pad, "Goal."

Before you start a safe
diet, set a realistic
goal.

Slides	*Narration*
Same legal pad showing woman's goal.	Decide the number of pounds within a period of time.
Cartoon of a woman trying to get to refrigerator, her husband and children barring entry.	When you start to diet, you will feel hungry.
Woman with salad, choosing between lemon juice and blue cheese dressing.	Learn to separate hunger from appetite.
Cartoon of woman at table with small plate of food.	Remember this: Less food is needed to satisfy hunger than is needed to appease appetite.
Cartoon of woman with a number of plates, small portions on each.	Space your meals to your own preference.
Chart saying "Breakfast," "Lunch," "Dinner," and "Snack," with denotation of number of calories at each.	Divide your daily food allowance into several smaller meals.
Second chart saying total number of calories.	It is the total calorie intake that counts.
Photo of foods.	Eat a wide variety of foods to keep the diet interesting.
Photo of fruits.	Fresh fruits and vegetables should be included.
Photo of raw vegetables.	Uncooked foods are higher in bulk and provide a satisfying feeling.
Photo of low-calorie foods.	Select low-calorie foods that allow a moderate-sized serving.
Photo of lettuce, celery, raw mushrooms.	Plan at least one food that may be eaten in an unlimited amount.
Type: Don't stop living!	Don't stop living.
Cartoon of woman at party.	Continue with your regular activities.

in store, looking at mirror, smiling.

Cartoon of woman sleeping.

Get plenty of sleep, especially in the first weeks.

Cartoon of woman digging in garden, planting rosebush.

Increase your ph, activity. This uses excess calories.

Repeat eighth visual.

There are seventy million Americans overweight.

Cartoon of obese woman walking to mailbox, yet putting out lots of effort.

An overweight woman's heart works harder with the extra weight.

Cartoon of same obese woman asleep at mailbox.

An overweight woman tires easily. She has less energy.

Cartoon of obese woman with ill-fitting clothes.

An overweight woman feels uncomfortable in her clothes.

Split-frame cartoon—left, cheerleader; right, same woman, older, heavier.

Some argue putting on pounds is a process of age.

*Type:
No excuse!*

It may be true, but it is no excuse.

Miracle-diet magazine ad photo with "top-secret" type red stamp over it, saying "BUNK!"

There are no miracle diets.

Safe diet + sensible exercise = weight loss

A safe diet, with sensible exercise, ensures weight loss.

*Type over visual:
"Common sense" over photo of happy woman.*

It's just common sense.

This fast-paced slide presentation uses 97 slides. Depending on the speaker, it runs from ten to fifteen minutes. It's flexible in that slides can be added or deleted, depending on the time alloted and the audience. It is designed so that a section on exercise and another on behavior modification can be added. The additional frames fit between the cartoon of the woman doing her gardening and the slide with the words, "70 million" (p. 115, fourth frame down):

Slides	*Narration*
Type: *Behavior modification*	Behavior modification. teaches the dieter to change harmful attitudes toward eating.
Obese woman on couch with Freud-like psychiatrist.	Psychological aspects of food consumption are explained.
Cartoon of child cleaning plate, mother standing over her sternly.	Many overweight adults were taught to clean their plates as children.
Cartoon of woman in chains, shackled to a big roast turkey.	This continues throughout adult life. The woman is psychologically enslaved.
Cartoon of woman at office stuffing candy in mouth, pop can nearby.	Women who feel pressure or stress may overeat.
Cartoon of woman out to lunch ordering a martini.	Another problem is when a dieter reaches her goal and relaxes.
Cartoon of same woman trying to zip zipper.	She regains all that lost weight.
Photo of discussion group.	These habits and attitudes can be changed through behavior modification.
Cartoon of woman at romantic, candlelight dinner.	Take time with your meal. Eat slowly. Savor each morsel.
Cartoon of same woman chewing.	Chew each bite a minimum of ten times.
Cartoon of one bite left on plate.	Leave at least one bite on the plate.

Visual	Narration
Cartoon of young children running around.	Avoid tense and hectic surroundings while you eat.
Photo of TV set.	Do not watch TV or listen to the radio while eating.
Photo of set table.	All food—even a sandwich—should be eaten with utensils.
Cartoon of woman counting on fingers, clock at 6 P.M.	After each bite, put down utensils, and count to ten.
Cartoon of same woman at table, clock says 8 P.M.	This breaks your eating pattern and slows you down.
Cartoon of discouraged woman on a large Toledo fortune scale.	Do not get discouraged: weight loss is unsteady.
Cartoon of woman angrily throwing bathroom scale out window.	For the first few days, weight loss is not noticed on the scale.

These additional fourteen slides and narration specifically on exercise make the point about the benefits of exercising, no matter what the age. The additional section includes photos, diagrams, and cartoons in the same style as the other visuals in the presentation.

Summary

The pace of both slide and film presentations is vital. There must be a balance: not too fast, but certainly not too slow. If the visual is too fast, the audience fails to grasp the full impact. If too slow, the audience becomes bored.

Writers (especially those who are print oriented) have a tendency to over-write both in film and slides. You must remember that the visual side dominates. Meticulously edit down all additional words out of the narration. In this way, your presentation will run smoothly and effectively, allowing a few well-chosen words to do the job.

The company publication

Most organizations employing more than a hundred people publish a newspaper or magazine. These publications vary widely. Some are run-off inexpensively on a mimeograph; others are printed in color with five-figure budgets and rival many of the consumer magazines in appearance. Publication schedules vary from monthly, bimonthly, to weekly.

The company publication, whether modest or elaborate, usually is the responsibility of the public relations practitioner, or, in a large corporation, the public relations department. Not only does the practitioner or assistant gather and write the news, but he also "makes up" the pages, supervises the printing, and follows through on the distributing.

No matter what the budget or printing quality of the house organ, there are certain rules that must be established before the first issue is printed.

119

Stylebook

All newspapers, magazines, and wire services have a stylebook. It determines the spelling of certain words, how titles and department names are written, and what words can be abbreviated.

Many newspapers throughout the country follow the *New York Times* stylebook (it is considered on a level with the Bible in many city rooms). However, everything in it is not pertinent to a company publication. So, it is best that the company practitioner-editor write a stylebook. The editor's first decision is how to treat employees' names. Will only first names be used, whether the employee is the chief executive officer or the newest edition to the mailroom? Or will the publication use the full name of executives and the first name of nonsupervisory personnel? Will *Mr., Mrs., Miss,* or *Ms.* be used? Most editors agree that it is good practice to use these titles, as the employee prefers. In this method the subject of the story is identified in the beginning as *Joyce J. Jones, Director of Marketing* and is referred to as *Ms., Miss,* or *Mrs. Jones* (as she prefers) during the rest of the story. Other publications use titles only for top executives and board members.

House organs boost employee morale, giving them a sense of belonging. As such, always respect the dignity of an employee, no matter what his station or status.

Journalistic style

Company publications tend to be slightly formal in editorial style. Employees are referred to by their full names, including middle initial, position, and department.

The style of writing is journalistic—factual—although there are certain traces of informality. Usually the smaller the company, the more informal the style. As the company grows, the style becomes more formal.

Layout

Size

The average tabloid newspaper is approximately 17 inches deep and 11¼ inches wide. The printed page, with borders on all four sides, is 15½ inches deep and 10 inches wide.

see p. 61), and the column width is 1¾ inches (10 picas wide—6 picas to an inch). A space slightly over ½ inch (2 picas wide) is allowed between columns.

If body copy is set in 10 point (the actual size of the type in the text of the story, allowing approximately 5 words to the printed line), one column takes approximately 565 words. Five columns, or a full page of solid type, takes 2,825 words.

The page will not be all type; there will be headlines, illustrations, photos, captions, and even, in some cases, diagrams. With headlines for stories, photos, and illustrations, the editor plans 2,000 words a page. In a 12-page newspaper, 24,000 words are needed.

A paper is two weeks of solid work. A typewritten page, double spaced, contains approximately 300 words, so you will need to write approximately 80 pages of copy.

Creating visual interest

Photographs break up the visual monotony of solid type on a page. The paste-up artist can also visually "dress up" a page by using different typefaces for headlines and decorative (and functional) rules.

You can add variety by setting some of the features used in each edition two columns wide. You can put a one-column head on one story, while giving others a two- or three-column head.

Page one

Page one, the front page, is the most important page of the newspaper. Because it is the first page read, it introduces the edition to the reader.

Put your most important stories on page one, with the story with the most impact—the story that affects the company the most—as the lead story. Sometimes the lead story is important enough to warrant a substantial headline—three, four, or even five columns across the page. Place the headline for the lead directly under the publication's name.

The editor and paste-up artist decide how the front page is made up. There are many different techniques for doing this. (See 8-2, p. 124.) At one time the first page lead had to run underneath the headline, down the right-hand column. Now it is not unusual to paste the lead story underneath the five-column headline, starting the text of the story in the left-hand column and running it across the page, column to column. In this method, there are fewer stories and the page isn't as broken up.

N. J. court rules against Nationwide

TRENTON, N.J.—Nationwide said it was giving "strong consideration" to appealing to the U.S. Supreme Court a New Jersey high court ruling that the company must renew no-fault auto insurance coverages as long as it has a license in the state.

In a 5-1 decision — one justice did not take part — the New Jersey Supreme Court turned aside Nation-wide's argument that requiring a company to renew auto policies which are causing financial losses is a violation of a company's constitutional rights.

The court said this week that its ruling does not apply to Nationwide's fire insurance company, which has no auto insurance business in New Jersey. That company can continue to non-renew business and still retain its license in the state.

Nationwide announced 21 months ago that because of losses in New Jersey, it would phase out its property-casualty insurance operations in the state. Its policy count there has since dropped steadily despite legal maneuvering.

The company was blocked from non-renewing auto policies in 1978 when the New Jersey insurance department obtained an injunction against the process.

Nationwide and other companies in New Jersey can non-renew no-fault auto coverages for certain specified reasons, or with the consent of the insurance commissioner.

There are no plans to surrender the auto company license in the state.

Nationwide® Times

Vol. 2, No. 26   July 19, 1979

PUBLISHED BY NATIONWIDE INSURANCE, COLUMBUS, OHIO

Emily and friends

The lady in the middle will visit the Plaza Wednesday from 11 a.m. to 12:30 p.m., as a preliminary to Nationwide Zoo Day Aug. 4. Tickets for the event — at $1.50 and 50 cents — are on sale in Activities. Here Emily — THE CHIMP — patronizes Zoo Day committee people Jim Coolbaugh (left) and Alex Gonzales.

It's cool to be warm: 78° change accepted

It was the feeling of the property management department that things went "pretty well" during the first two days of Nationwide's change to 78 degrees in its four Columbus buildings — the Plaza, 246 N. High St., 35 E. Chestnut St., and the Training Center.

"We didn't get nearly as many complaints as we expected," said a spokesman. "Generally, people seemed to accept the change. They cooperated with us and we're trying to do the same with them."

Property management acknowledged that there were problems in the Plaza pavilion and the Medicare CRT area of the tower, but said that it was "fine tuning" there and in other locations to bring temperatures down from around 80 to 78.

Engineers faced a difficulty as they began to prepare the buildings for change last Friday: increased heat over the weekend. They worked around the clock into Monday morning to alter indoor temperatures that had been between 73 and 74 degrees.

That meant resetting every building's thermostats, and property management said that it was pleased that there had been almost no efforts since to set thermostats back to original readings. Tampering with the mechanisms is against federal law.

The problem in the pavilion, said property management, was that there was some air movement, but not enough. The first couple of hours Monday were particularly difficult everywhere, and that will probably continue because building systems are shut down over the weekends.

Employee health services reported, however, that fewer than 10 persons visited there Monday with possible heat-related conditions.

Nationwide's buildings are cooled for air-conditioning by "centrifugal chillers," each of 1,600-ton capacity. The energy-saving occurs simply by using less power to operate the chillers. They are turned off each day a half-hour after regular working hours. They go back on in time for the buildings to reach 78 degrees by the time the next work day begins.

Incidentally, the buildings will remain at 78 degrees during the cooling season, regardless of outdoor temperatures.

Life policy sales hit $1 billion earlier than ever

Agents' awareness of increasing customer needs helped spur life insurance sales to the $1 billion mark earlier than at any time in the company's' history.

Sales hit $1 billion July 11, said director of life marketing C. J. (Chuck) Mathews. "In the past, the earliest we hit $1 billion was in October," Mathews added.

A total of 51,000 policies were sold.

A combination of factors was responsible for the achievement, Mathews said.

The introduction of three new life products in August, 1978, started the ball rolling. Those products included a new yearly renewable-term, "mini-mal-issue" $50,000 policy, a new mortgage-protection contract with significant rate reductions, and an additional insured rider that enables a policy to cover more than one person under a single contract.

More important, said Mathews, was agents' "increasing awareness of customer needs due to inflation, and an increased awareness of serving the total needs of customers. Because of inflation, the average policy we sell today is for $20,000. Before double digit inflation, many customers purchased about $10,000 worth of life coverage."

Added agent emphasis on life insurance, said Mathews, is an aspect of "rekindled interest in selling our total 'package'," which includes auto and fire protection. In support of that, there seems to be growing customer approval of having one agent handle all their needs.—C.A.R.

CPCU annual meeting info now available

Persons who wrote their last CPCU exam in January or June and who plan to attend the Annual Meeting and Conferment in Boston in September should contact Rick Braschel in personnel development, ext. 6199, in order to receive registration information.

The requested deposit must be remitted to CPCU to secure a room.

Services pending for W. John Blackstone

Funeral services were pending yesterday morning for W. John Blackstone, 62, general attorney in the office of general counsel, who died Tuesday following a heart attack suffered at his home.

Blackstone had been with the company since 1948.

Boards elect McFerson VP—internal audits

Election by the boards of D. Richard McFerson as vice president-internal audits has been announced by President Fisher. The appointment is effective Sept. 3.

For the past six years McFerson has been senior vice president and controller of the New England Mutual Life Insurance Company.

Mr. Fisher said that management staffing in the office of internal audits will include D.E. Horstick as data processing audits manager, Julius M. Palenski as insurance operations audits manager, and Robert M. Graham as non-insurance audits manager.

Indicating that McFerson will be directly responsible to him, Mr. Fisher said that the appointment recognizes the increasing importance of the auditing function.

He also said it is "in accordance with an emerging trend in U.S. industry to have independent separation of internal audits from other financial activities within a corporate structure."

Such moves, the president affirmed, have been encouraged by the Securities & Exchange Commission and other state and federal regulatory bodies.

Figure 8–1. Example of a four-column tabloid. Note the variety of typefaces and graphics.

A photo accompanying the lead story can be run five columns wide if it has enough drama or impact to warrant that much exposure on the page.

Dummy

The page is "dummied" after the selection of stories and photographs. A dummy is a rough, pencil sketch of page one, indicating visually how the page will appear when printed.

The dummy is a guide for the paste-up artist. Some editors dummy each page, while others allow the paste-up artist to fit the stories and photos in on various pages.

Most regular features, such as the president's letter, is run in a standard place each issue. The president's column is usually run underneath the masthead on page two. (The masthead gives the name of the publication, the name and address of the company, and lists the editor's name and those on the staff. It is usually two columns wide and placed on the left side on page two at the top.)

As the stories come in from the departments, the editor may find that some material may need rewriting. Some writers are too basic, others too flowery. One of the ways to solve this problem is to give each correspondent a form that covers all the pertinent information needed to write the story. He fills out the form and the editor writes the story.

You should realize that some managements view the company publication as a propaganda vehicle. They want employees to know only certain aspects of the company's operation. When a newspaper wins a reputation as a propaganda sheet for management, readership is minimal. The company publication should be a communication tool and morale builder. Management must understand the need for a legitimate, objective publication respected by employees. This goal is not impossible. An editor must be strong and not yield to unwarranted management demands. If the publication is not read by employees, it is a waste of money, time, and effort; a chief executive officer seldom can ignore that argument.

Editorial content

The content of each publication differs; the format reflects the news taste and judgment of the editor and, to some extent, the management. Many publications start informally as a mimeographed sheet with no guidelines on what is considered news. As the publication progresses to a full-blown company newspaper, editorial guidelines are hammered out through trial and error. A paper that started out saying, "Good old Harry in the shipping room is a grandfather" usually progresses to a formal, "Harry S. Brown of the Shipping Department recently became a grandfather."

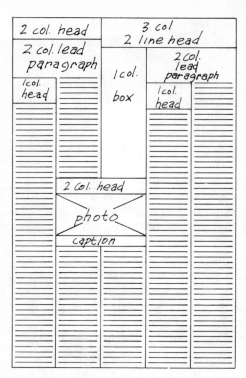

Figure 8–2.

Traditional 5-column.

Modern method.

As the publication ages, problems with space allotment grow. Most editors are "tight" for space, and such problems as whether to include the bowling league scores must be dealt with.

Personnel employees advocate including personal notes (birthdays, graduations) for morale purposes; other employees, especially those in the financial department, may term such notes "a terrible waste of space." It is true that graduation time can become an editor's nightmare, with lists of graduating children and even grandchildren.

As an editor, you should have a consistent content policy: the bowling scores are run in the winter, then the golf league scores are printed in the summer. If a story is written about the marriage of a vice-president's daughter, the assistant manager's daughter's marriage should be given space.

Editors attempt to balance their coverage with news about the company and interesting features about the company, personnel, and the industry.

Some editors make an effort to have each department, branch, and division represented in a story or column each edition. Other editors hold to the policy of mentioning only those areas in which there is a legitimate story.

Deadlines

As with any publication printed on a regular basis, there must be a deadline for editorial content. It takes approximately four weeks for publication of a tabloid-size, twelve-page newspaper. This schedule includes getting the news, taking pictures, writing stories, making up the pages, printing the paper, and distributing the edition.

It will take you about two weeks to gather the news, take pictures and write the copy. You will edit the copy, mark it for size (one column, two column, etc.), and insert appropriate headlines. You then send it to the typesetter. You will receive galley proofs, which you return for correction to the typesetter. The typesetter supplies repro galleys for an artist to paste up into pages of camera-ready copy. The artist may be working for the typesetter, the public relations department, or freelance. The pages are then reread for any last-minute corrections or alterations. The printer usually takes a week to print the paper.

Examples of stories

The Davis Insurance Company, with 2,000 employees, puts out a monthly newspaper. It is a traditional tabloid, five columns wide, eight pages long. (See Figure 8-3, p. 126.)

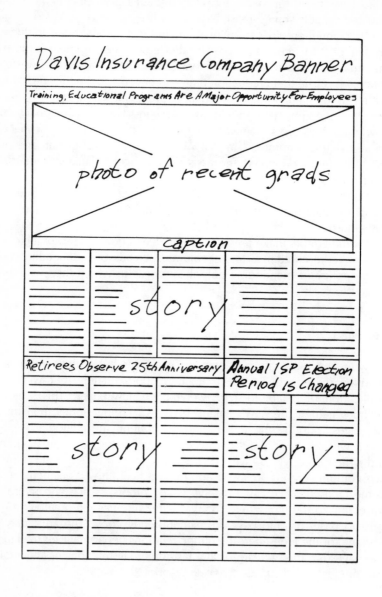

Figure 8–3. Traditional monthly newspaper.

Its news format is employee oriented. It uses many photos; the lead story on page one usually has a photo. Page one also contains two other stories.

The main headline in the issue we'll look at is "Training, Educational Programs Are a Major Opportunity for Employees." This page one headline runs in one line across five columns. The story, set in one column, starts on the left-hand column and runs three inches deep, in sequence, in each of the five columns. A photograph of recent graduates is included, five columns wide.

The story:

One of the most rewarding opportunities afforded employees is the company's program for advanced training and development.

The Career Educational Program of the Personnel Department offers employees courses and programs suited to both individual and company needs.

These programs are designed to provide skills, techniques, and concepts that will enhance an employee's growth and development and improve his or her organizational effectiveness.

The popularity of the programs is tangibly shown by the enrollment figures.

A total of 467 employees enrolled for courses this September. This figure represents the highest number of enrollments in the history of the program, now in its 10th year.

The individual courses and programs include business skills, presupervisory courses, supervisory and management courses, personnel policies and procedures, modern concepts of management, and special seminars.

There is a program known as the *curriculum commitment*. Employees make a three-year commitment to a group of related courses at the secretarial, pre-supervisory, or management level.

This concept is designed to enable an employee to follow a "career path" within the company.

Training consultant services are available to employees. Members of the teaching staff work with individuals and departments on special training needs.

Insurance education programs designed by outside organizations are offered to employees on a self-study basis. These organizations include Life Office Management Association, Health Insurance Association of America, Chartered Life Underwriters, and Academy of Life Underwriters.

The tuition award program is an outstanding opportunity. The company encourages employee growth and development by offering incentives for successful completion of courses at accredited two- and four-year educational institutions.

Information about the education and training programs is found in the education and training catalog. The personnel policies and procedures manual, which lists courses, is available to all employees.

A time and room schedule is distributed to all employees before the start of each academic term. In addition, special announcements are published in the career educational bulletin and in this newspaper.

Two other stories are on page one: "Retirees Observe 25th Anniversary" and "Annual ISP Investment Election Period Is Changed." The retirees story headline has a one-line, three-column head, and the other story has a two-column, two-line head.

The retirees story:

A record number of retired employees met to attend their annual luncheon at the company home office on September 26th.

Chairman of the Board Harris welcomed everyone, noting that he will be at the luncheon as a retiree next year.

President Black commented on the burgeoning attendance at the luncheon and said, "Although no attendance records were kept for the 1955–56 luncheons, in 1957, we had 129 retirees attend the third annual luncheon.

"Today there are 534 retirees present. There are 713 retirees, and 338 of that number are seventy-five years old or older."

The president paid special tribute to Wanda Kirsten, who recently retired from the personnel department.

At the close of the luncheon, President Black extended the customary invitation to the retirees to visit their friends and colleagues in their former work areas.

The investment election change story:

Incentive-savings plan participants will receive their third-quarter statement this week.

Participants also will receive a notice and change forms for making investment election changes and for the transfer of shares between funds.

The notice will explain in detail all options open to participants. For those who wish more information or who wish to join the company's incentive-savings plan, please contact the plan office.

None of these three stories continue on another page. On page two is the president's message and one column on employee promotions, including photographs (head and shoulders) of those promoted. Each promotion announcement mentions the person's name, department, the new position, and the person's background. Here's an example:

Mary T. O'Brien has been promoted to manager of the Issue Service Division.

In her new post Ms. O'Brien will provide managerial direction for the department. The division is responsible for the daily analysis, inspection, and mailing of all individual life and annuity policies.

She has completed a number of LOMA studies and has attended various company supervisory and management courses.

On page three, there are two stories: "Health Clinic to Begin Flu Innoculations," and "Why Give to United Way?" Two photographs were used on page three, one showing a medical researcher, and the other, a photograph of the Red Cross in action at a major fire.

The innoculation story:

The Health Clinic announces that the Influenza Program, a routine part of the company's health maintenance program, will have two projects.

Part One—ages 26 and over.

Part Two—ages 25 and under.

This change is due to the appearance of a major variant of a Type A virus. This virus appeared in Russia and China, and it may be related to strains that have circulated throughout the world in the early 1950s.

People over the age of 25 were not affected. Those 25 and under were affected in outbreaks in schools, industry, and the community.

The Health Clinic will proceed with Part One of the Influenza Program at this time. As soon as the proper vaccine arrives, the Part Two program will start.

Only one dose is required for the Part One program.

Identification and authorization cards will be distributed along with paychecks. These cards will be collected prior to innoculation.

Also with paychecks will be written notice as to the date and time of each employee's appointment for innoculation.

Naturally this program is on a voluntary basis, but the Public Health Service and the Health Clinic's staff strongly recommend that all employees take advantage of this free service.

This program is especially important for employees with acquired or congenital heart disease, chronic pulmonary disorders, chronic kidney disease, diabetes mellitus, and chronic anemia.

Innoculation for older persons, especially those over 65, is recommended by medical experts.

Health Clinic doctors point out that employees allergic to chicken, chicken feathers, or eggs should not get the flu shot unless so advised by their personal physician.

Preliminary tests have indicated few side effects for most people. There have been some limited local reactions of redness and swelling and a small number of systematic reactions with mild fever, aches, and malaise.

The Guillian-Barre syndrome, an uncommon illness, is mentioned because last year there was an increased incidence of 10 cases for every million persons innoculated.

This incidence was five to six times that reported in unvaccinated persons. There is no comparable information about the association of this disease with other influenza vaccines.

The risk was extremely low. The risk, however, should be balanced against the risk of influenza and its complications.

Should you have any questions, check with the staff at the Health Clinic or your physician.

The United Way story:

As a community resident, you are asked to contribute to the United Way appeal.

Why is your pledge so important?

Chances are that you or your family already use the services of a United Way member agency.

There are 162 agencies that depend on the United Way campaign for support.

One out of every four persons in 66 cities and towns will be helped by an United Way member agency through a wide variety of regular programs or emergency services.

The most dramatic evidence of the United Way in action was last year's blizzard.

Thousands of people were left homeless and badly in need of food and shelter. Many were stranded.

The Red Cross responded immediately. "Visiting nurses" plowed through snow drifts to assist shut-ins.

Neighborhood centers provided shelter around the clock. The Salvation Army offered food and clothing.

Even the Boy Scouts helped motorists stuck for miles along the inner-belt. These and other agencies responded when they were needed.

Now, these agencies ask you to help them.

Other emergencies? One never knows when an accident or fire might strike. Or when a youngster may need special help.

Your United Way contribution helps produce trained volunteers to treat heart attack victims, take blood donations, and be Big Brothers and Big Sisters.

All of us will grow old. United Way agencies provide many services for the elderly, healthy or homebound.

For example, Visiting Nurses helped more than 24,000 people last year. The majority of these people were old and needed help at home.

Some of us need a little extra help in life. Seven United Way agencies provide sheltered workshops, physical therapy, camping opportunities, and training centers.

More than 800 physically and mentally handicapped persons of all ages are helped by these agencies.

The 162 agencies provide a broad range of health, counseling, family, child care, or youth services. Please give generously.

At the end of the United Way story is a one-paragraph story with a rule (border) around it with the headline: "Employees Featured in Slide Show."

The paragraph:

Employees visiting United Way agencies will be featured in a slide show at the employee's cafeteria during the lunch period all next week. The United Way Committee, in cooperation with the Corporation Television Center, will present the slide show.

Page four contains five stories of various company events and happenings as well as a feature headlined "Safety First."

The story:

At today's speeds, motorists must pay full attention to driving.

And yet, all of us are guilty in doing the following things while driving that, in a split second, could cause an accident:

Fastening your seat belt
Finding and counting the exact change for a toll road pay station
Searching for a toll ticket
Lighting a cigarette
Tuning the radio
Setting a watch or dashboard clock
Handling eye or sunglasses
Minding the children
Consulting a map
Making a seat or mirror adjustment

Page five contains a layout of photographs, with a five-column, one-line headline: "Company Honors Its Quarter Century Club Members." The twelve photographs are identified in one giant caption.

Page six and seven include company-oriented feature stories, including an employee-sponsored trip to London and a theatre party.

The back page, eight, lists free classified ads, including ads for automobiles and furniture for sale, housing, rides wanted, a lost and found section, and a notice for free kittens. Office phone changes of personnel are noted, as well as a job opportunity column containing descriptions of job openings within the company.

The writing style is a bit informal. No personal notes are included because the company is too big. One column does list weddings but does not include stories or wedding photographs. Obituaries of employees and former employees are printed. Retirement stories are given a prominent position. The promotion column is a monthly feature.

The company magazine

You may be in a position where you must edit or start a magazine without a staff. Such magazines usually contain feature stories, other stories pertinent to the company's operation, and a personnel section.

Size

Magazines are printed in multiples of 4 pages. Most small magazines run from 16 to 24 pages. The page size is 11 inches deep and 8 inches wide. The page format usually is 3 columns wide, 10½ inches deep. Column width is 2½ inches wide. Depth is 70 lines. There are 350 words per column, 1050 words to a 3-column page. Thus to fill a magazine page you need to write 3½ typewritten pages, double spaced.

A twenty-page magazine takes 60,000 words, with the front and back cover not being used for editorial content. This figure also takes into consideration the president's column, photographs, headlines, the masthead, and even a cartoon or two.

Art and feature sources

There are services that supply magazine materials from which you can buy general interest feature stories, stock photographs, and illustrations.

Some services can supply free feature stories, complete with photographs. These stories usually deal with an industry or a segment of an industry and are well written and generally interesting.

There are graphic houses such as Dynamic Graphics in Peoria, Illinois, who supply camera-ready stock cover designs, holiday themes, headings, symbols, and other design and graphic elements to dress up the publication. The editor, without the services of an artist, can function as a make-up editor with the aid of these "clip" art services.

Ashland News

Volume XIX   June 1979   Number 6

Coming soon -- A special issue on gasoline supply and pricing

Inside:

The summer of '79 has become the season of shortage as rising consumer gasoline demand collides with a worldwide crude oil shortfall. The call for motor fuel is up 3.9 percent this year over 1978, while crude oil stocks remain low. Stories, pages 2 and 3.

Figure 8–4. This *Ashland News* cover uses a photo and reversed type out of a black band. Articles inside discuss oil, employee promotions, job stress, and driving tips.

Organization

The front cover is considered page one, followed by the president's message on the inside front cover, page two. Page three is the masthead and contents page, and page four contains a column such as personal notes. Depending on variations of this order, the lead may begin on page three or five, but always on a right-hand page.

Pages ten and eleven of a twenty-page magazine are used by some editors for miscellaneous photographs (those pictures without stories).

Figure 8–5. The company magazine shown on the next four pages is published four times a year by Ashland's financial communications department. In this issue, printed in full color, the theme of the major article is introduced on the cover and contents page.

ASHLANDNOW

Summer 1979
Volume 3, Number 2

Cover: A traditional
avian symbol of the sea,
brown pelicans soar
above the Louisiana
coastline. Photograph by
Dan Guravich.

Contents

Melinda H. Hamilton
Editor

Teo Nutini
Corporate Advertising Director

James H. Marsh
Art Director

Larry R. Borton
Associate Art Director

ASHLAND NOW is published four times a year by the Financial
Communications Department of Ashland Oil, Inc. It is produced for
Ashland's stockholders, employees and friends.
Registered In The United States Patent and Trademark Office.

Permission to reprint material and change of address requests may be
directed to ASHLAND NOW. Financial Communications Department, Ashland Oil, Inc., Box 391, Ashland, Kentucky 41101.

1

The back inside cover is excellent for classified ads, and the outside back cover is left open for the name and address of the employee if the publication is to be mailed.

Content

The Davis Insurance Company also publishes a quarterly magazine, twenty-four to twenty-eight pages, directed to the independent insurance agents in this country and Canada. Their magazine features a full-color photograph on the cover followed by the president's column.

Cajun country's "grand gosier"

By Joseph E. Brown

He's a big, comical, awkward bird, even ugly, some insist. Sheer poetry in flight, soaring effortlessly on wind currents or "troughing" between ocean swells, he is the original Mr. Clumsy on land, stumbling as he does over his webbed feet as he wobbles around on his island nesting ground.

His beak is a caricaturist's delight. Extending 18 inches at maturity, it is a useful tool when diving for food for himself and his even uglier hatchling young. But it is a gargantuan appendage compared to body size and, according to Dixon Lanier Merritt's popular but scientifically incorrect 1910 limerick, it

"can hold more fish than his belly-can."

Though we may poke fun at him, the laughable brown pelican—*pelicanus occidentalis* to the ornithologist, *grand gosier* ("big gullet") to the Louisiana Cajun fisherman whose habitat he shares among others—is one of the most remarkable birds on earth.

One of two New World pelican species (the other is the closely related white pelican) and one of only six in the entire world, he is, for one thing, a spectacular fish-catcher. Spotting his prey from high aloft, he rarely misses his target, correcting his downward plummet with flicks

of wing and tail and guiding himself by aim of his monstrous beak.

Pelicans are also good parents. In their three major American habitats—California, Louisiana and Florida—they fiercely defend their nests against predators (egg-stealing gulls are a particular nuisance) even at the risk of harm to themselves. One old legend insists, in fact, that mother pelicans are so protective that occasionally one will tear open her own breast to feed her young with blood when other food is unavailable.

Mostly, however, it is the brown pelican's hardy durability that has made him so admirable, and such a

2

traditional avian symbol of the sea. Scarcely changed at all in the eons of animal evolution, the pelican was a pelican long before man became man. Fossil evidence dates this bird back at least 30 or 40 million years. Considering that since the first bird evolved from a reptile-like creature and took wing, nature has experimented with and then discarded all but 8,000 of a total of 2,000,000 bird species that earth has known, the pelican deserves its reputation as one of earth's most lasting creatures, a bird with a seemingly infinite capability of self-survival.

One can understand, then, the shock wave that rippled through Louisiana in the early 1960s when ornithologists learned that the brown pelican had vanished from their state. Old records indicate that as late as the 1930s, the population of Louisiana's official state bird had numbered nearly 50,000, perhaps as high as 85,000. But in 1961 when scientist G. F. Van Tets visited a former nesting site in the Chandeleur Islands, not a single pelican could be found.

Laymen as well as scientists were astonished. The sight of the friendly bird, perched on wharf pilings, snitching fish, or gracefully winging its way across the bayou country, had become as taken-for-granted a

An endangered species, the brown pelican is flourishing once again on the Louisiana coast with the petroleum industry as its neighbor.

3

Most companies, national or international in scope, with subsidiary companies or a number of plants or branch offices, publish such a company magazine. Some are monthly, others quarterly.

The larger the corporation, the more sophisticated the publication. Most of these magazines have a full-time editor, one or two staff writers, and a staff photographer.

The Davis Company magazine includes two feature stories, which will be illustrated here. The first story about a company employee includes two pages of photographs of the employee and his electric car.

It Only Costs 1¢ a Mile

If you find yourself driving down the highway, easily passing a blue Volkswagen emblazoned with the name *Electric Bug,* don't laugh.

It may be slow but it costs only one cent per mile to run.

The electric-powered car is owned by Harry Jones, who is a draftsman/designer with our company.

Mr. Jones converted the car's standard transmission several months ago and regularly drives the vehicle to work.

His "Electric Bug" can reach a speed of fifty miles per hour for a distance of approximately fifty miles. Twelve six-volt truck batteries, an industrial charger, and a seven horsepower electric motor provide the fuel.

Mr. Jones charges the batteries, the car's only maintenance, through a regular electric outlet for six hours. He uses fifty cents worth of electricity, which averages out to one cent a mile.

This expense compares with the cost of approximately four cents a mile for a regular Volkswagen and seven cents for a standard-sized automobile.

When Mr. Jones takes the Bug to work, he recharges the batteries for the trip home through an outlet installed for him at his parking space.

Cost of the conversion was $1,500, including $1,400 for parts and $100 for the Volkswagen.

It took Mr. Jones approximately forty hours to complete the conversion from gas to electricity. He took out the back seat to set up the batteries: three in front, nine in back; then he cut holes for the generator.

He hooked the motor into the transmission.

Mr. Jones said the Volkswagen was especially good to work with because the power source was in the rear. And he feels any handy person with reasonable intelligence could do the same thing.

He hasn't experienced any difficulties as yet. It is pollution free and quiet, with just a slight whirring noise. His family also owns a gas-powered car.

Mr. Jones first started to think about the possibilities of an electric car when he was in Amsterdam, a city that already has electric cars for hire.

When he returned home, Mr. Jones contacted an electric transportation company. They provided him with a set of instructions and a list of essential parts.

He worked nights and weekends for a month, a total of 40 hours, before the car was ready to go.

Most people's reaction to his "Electric Bug" is first amusement and then curiosity. A number have offered to buy it and one man wanted to go into the electric car business with him.

Mr. Jones said, "I already have a job. I did it for my own entertainment; I get a lot of fun out of it. And I know what I can accomplish."

The second story is as follows:

Company Sponsors CPR Training

Could you save someone having a heart attack?

Or would you watch hopelessly as the victim dies before your eyes?

When tragedy strikes, you have only four to six minutes to save a person suffering from cardiac arrest. This year 750,000 Americans will die from heart attacks.

With CPR (cardiopulmonary resuscitation) training, you would know what to do.

A trained person, acting quickly and knowledgeably, can save a life.

Now you can learn these valuable skills through a company-sponsored program. The local Red Cross chapter is providing an instructor and our company is providing space. The company has purchased a full set of mannequins for use in the training.

Classes will be held each Monday evening for six weeks from 5 to 6 o'clock. Employees signing up will be trained to use a combination of mouth-to-mouth resuscitation and chest compression.

The more employees who learn these functions, the better the chance that help will be available when the unexpected strikes. All those employees who successfully pass the course will be awarded certificates.

It is hoped that at least a third of our employees take this valuable training. The life you save may be a friend or loved one.

Summary

The company publication is a valuable communication tool for the company. It must be written and edited with the employees firmly in focus—interesting and informative, not propaganda from management.

Newsletters

One of the oldest and most time-honored forms of group communication is the newsletter. Literally thousands of such letters are printed and distributed by various organizations. From the small village parish, garden club, and bowling league to the trade association or union with thousands of members, newsletters are written, printed, and mailed. They are an efficient and inexpensive way to communicate to a specific group.

Newsletters are done in various forms. Some are typed like a letter on a plain sheet of paper, run-off on a copying machine, placed in a regular business-sized envelope and mailed.

Others, especially those produced for large trade associations, unions, and other formally structured organizations, are more professional in appearance and content. Some include photographs, have a masthead, and use more of a journalistic writing style.

Some newsletters are hand distributed, while others are placed in an envelope and mailed; but most newsletters leave a third of the back page blank for the address and postage. Nonprofit organizations may obtain a nonprofit mailing permit and save on postage. Others obtain bulk permits.

Do not confuse an organization's newsletter with company reports. These reports detail company services, investments, current legislation in the field, and business and industrial trends. They are sent out weekly, biweekly, or monthly.

Style

Most newsletters are journalistic in style and range from informal to formal depending on the organization and its audience. As the organization grows in size and status, so does the formality of the writing and content of the newsletter.

As previously mentioned, a stylebook assures consistency in spelling, the use of names, and figures and dates of meetings. This manual does not have to be formal, but it should be written so that the typist, proofreader, writers, and editor know the style and have something to refer to.

Layout and schedule

The newsletter is the responsibility of the trade association's public relations practitioner. He decides on the format, gathers the material, writes the stories, and supervises the production. He is limited only by his budget and lack of imagination. Most associations publish a newsletter once a month. Two weeks is the usual time needed to write and print a four-page newsletter.

Each page of the average newsletter is 8½ inches wide by 11 inches deep. The overall size before the newsletter is folded into pages is 17 inches wide by 11 inches deep. When folded in the middle, there are 4 pages.

The newsletter is folded three times, in equal parts, each part being 3½ inches deep. The outside part (a third of page four, the back page) is used for the address and postage.

The copy is set across the page, 7 inches wide (42 picas). Approximately 15 words a line are needed for copy run across the page. Without too much white space and large headlines, 50 to 55 lines fill one page, 8 inches wide and 11½ inches deep. From 750 to 825 words fill a page. A 4-page newsletter needs 3,000 words of copy, using the 750 word per page approximation. This figure assumes a space (leading) is used between the lines of type.

You can make the page more readable by triple spacing between some news items; indenting margins 2½ or 3 inches instead of the customary ¾ inch; and by writing some lines in capitals. Headings in caps break up the monotony of a typewritten page. You can also make use of photos and clip art.

To give the newsletter more of an appearance of a newspaper than a letter, you can set the copy in two columns on the page. Other ideas for creating interest include printing in a color other than black; having a distinctive design for a masthead on the first page; using a screen (a tint of solid color behind the type) to emphasize a certain section of a story.

Examples of content

Two newsletters are illustrated here. The first newsletter is for a trade association; the second is for a union.

The association's masthead proclaims: "The Bay State Small Business Association." Its newsletter's lead headline, page one, is "Business Unites to Fight Classification."

The story:

> Classification, the first ballot question in this year's election, is being fought by a number of business and professional associations.
> Proposition One could well spell doom for Bay State small businesses.
> The Bay State Small Business Association has joined with hundreds of other businesses and industrial and professional associations in fighting this unfair proposition.
> An educational campaign employing mass media—radio, television, newspapers—has been launched by this coalition. The campaign tells the voter that Proposition One will not necessarily lower property taxes.
> All Proposition One does, if approved, is to allow the state legislature to classify property for tax purposes into four groups: industrial, business, apartment, and home.

Moving to a Mountain   Some Borden Inc. employees breathed a sigh of relief when the world's highest formaldehyde plant went into operation earlier this year at the 9,400-foot level in Quito, Ecuador.

Bringing the prefabricated plant from Seattle, Wash., to the heights of the South American country was a feat that some might have likened to dragging the last, heavy building block to the top of a pyramid.

For although the plant is small by definition of a manufacturing "plant," (it measured 37 feet long, 15 feet high and 12 feet wide, crated) it weighed a whopping 30 tons and had to be taken to its final location from sea level by truck.

Company officials got their first clue that getting the plant to its final resting place might not be easy when they received a call from port authorities saying the shipment had arrived, but nobody there seemed to have the papers that would allow it to be unloaded.

Upon examination of the situation, it was found that the plant had been shipped to the wrong port — 75 miles from its original destination. Worse yet, the port where the shipment arrived lacked facilities to handle such a large and weighty piece of freight.

Borden representatives tackled the problems of papers and clearances. They managed to get permission to transport the shipment on a trailer that was five feet shorter and five feet narrower than the box — but which was the largest one in the country. They arranged for five cranes to unload

A crate containing a formaldehyde plant makes its way up a mountain highway in the South American country of Ecuador. The entire shipment measured 37 by 15 by 12 feet and weighed 30 tons. While this is not an unusually heavy freight load ordinarily, the climb from sea level to 9,400 feet at Quito required the successive aid of three trucks because the heavy load caused vehicular failure.

Workmen take the formaldehyde plant out of its traveling crate. Built in Seattle, Wash., the unit traveled to Ecuador by ship before its 75-mile truck trip up the Andes Mountains. The plant holds the distinction of being the highest formaldehyde plant in the world.

the big box because no single crane in the country was equal to the task.

When it was found that the total height of the box on the truck was 16 feet, arrangements had to be made to send a team of five people ahead to cut more than 120 power lines, many of them crossing the road at a height of only about 13 feet. At one town of 3,000 population, the load was allowed to travel through only between 2 and 4 a.m. and only with the provision that 46 cables that had to be cut would be properly reconnected.

The weight of the load caused problems too. The bottom of the box was rubbing the tires and caused two to burst. It was a day before a heavy-duty jack could be brought in for tire repair and the box could be moved again. When the load faced a steep 60-mile climb into the Andes Mountains, the moving process began "using up" trucks. The first truck had traveled only ten miles, at six miles per hour,

constantly changing gears, before its clutch gave up. It was then decided to place trucks every 13 miles along the route, a strategy that paid off as the second truck broke down 33 miles from Quito with a replacement 20 minutes away.

The final climb to Quito proceeded at one mile per hour because of heavy fog on a narrow road full of traffic.

It took seven days, in all, to accomplish the moving task, and then the crews rested.

Left behind were piles of official papers full of signatures and stamps, more than 120 wire cuttings, two broken trucks and disappointed kids who thought the box meant a circus was coming to town.

Figure 9–1. Two pages from a ten-page, folded newsletter on a base sheet 9″ × 18″.

The proponents of this resolution say that it could lower real estate taxes. Home owners are protesting over high property taxes and, therefore, mistakenly believe Proposition One will give relief.

Actually, if approved, Proposition One would give the legislature a free reign to tax any of the four classifications any way they wish.

This state now has the highest taxes in the nation. Our businesses are paying the highest real estate taxes, the highest excise taxes on equipment, the highest income tax, the highest corporation taxes, and the highest sales tax.

The membership is urged to do everything possible to show the danger if Proposition One passes. And remember, your vote does count.

The President's message is on page two.

From the President's Desk

Small business needs a voice within the government.

On the federal level, the small business owner is represented by the Small Business Administration. Whether we in this state consider that agency an effective voice for small business is open to debate.

The fact remains that we do have some representation in Washington. There is someone speaking for small business.

We do not have representation at the State House. Small businesses are regulated by 50 different state agencies and administrations, but no one speaks for small business per se.

Small business by far is the largest single group in this state, out numbering the large corporations 1,000 to one. More than three quarters of all businesses in this state are considered in the small business category.

Without small business, the economy of this state could well grind to a halt. Thus it is vital that small business have a strong and effective voice at the State House.

The state Small Business Agency would not be a regulatory board. Its function would be to aid small businesses to prosper and to aid in the establishment of other small businesses.

Thousands of dollars are spent annually by the state's Department of Commerce and Department of Labor and Industries, advertising this area as the place to construct a new plant or office building.

Executives of large corporations are wined and dined by state officials in the hope that these executives will chose this state as the site of a new plant.

All types of tax advantages are offered to these companies if the management agrees to build here.

And yet, not one cent is spent to promote small businesses to come here. In fact, one would feel officials are intent in halting the establishment of the small business.

From the small restaurant owner in town to the operator of the service station on the corner, we are all small businesses.

It is time the small business was heard at the State House, both by the administration and the legislature.

We urge you to write your local state representative and senator and ask that such an agency be formed.

Sincerely,

John H. Jones, President

On page three of the newsletter is a report on federal legislation with the headline "Small Business Victory on Tax Legislation."

The tax measures approved by the Senate Finance Committee recently set the stage for the establishment of a graduated corporate income tax.

The Finance Committee recommends even more generous reductions in capital gains taxes than did the House. The final word on these proposals will be determined at the House/Senate conference.

The Senate Finance Committee called for reductions in the maximum rate of capital gains taxation to 25 percent and increased the capital gains exclusion from 50 to 70 percent.

The Committee followed the concept of targeting job tax credits to the hard-core unemployed.

The job tax credit issue involves the projected cost to the Treasury of such credit.

A motion to include provisions in the tax bill allowing for accelerated depreciation was voted on by the Committee.

In the asset depreciation method, a 30 percent increase was suggested by the Committee. This, of course, benefits big business. The three-year, straight-line write-off for the first $25,000 worth of equipment, which would be of real benefit to small business, was rejected.

The rest of the newsletter, written in a chatty style, is devoted to personal items about members and a list of those appointed to various committees of the association.

In a second example, the Utility Workers newsletter features union news and personal notes. Its lead headline is "Credit Union Board of Directors to Be Elected."

The story:

The Renco Employees' Credit Union will hold its annual election for Board of Directors on Tuesday, November 5 at the Renco Hall, Milton.

Voting will be from 7 A.M. to 8 P.M.

Local 999 has three candidates seeking election.

William P. Marston has been a member of the Board of Directors since 1960. He is seeking a 10th term.

Debra H. Hilton, secretary-treasurer of the local, is seeking re-election to her fourth term.

Dick King is seeking election for the first time. An Executive Board member, he offers wide experience.

The major issue is whether an employee of the credit union (those working in the office) should be able to serve as a director.

The three candidates take a strong position against this dual role.

They state that one of the functions of a director is the responsibility of supervising the office staff to insure that everyone—union and management—is treated with respect and dignity.

The three stated, "We believe a director working as an employee is an undesirable condition that could damage the credit union."

The knowledge and dedication of our directors, Marston and Hilton, have helped the union to become a leader among unions. The union now has $19,000,000 in assets.

Each union member is urged to elect our three members to the Board of Directors.

On page two, the headline reads "Operator Case Settled." The story:

A Board of Arbitration found the company to be in violation of the Collective Bargaining Agreement for actions that were protested in a grievance.

The Board of Arbitration met in Executive Session and the following facts were considered pertinent.

In the period following the date of the grievance, there were 56 separate violations.

In this period, there were 15 Grade A and 17 Grade B employees in the classification of Operation-Substation, at hourly rates of $8.35 and $8.01, respectively.

It is agreed that the overhaul work performed takes a full shift. The issue is whether the remedy should be based on eight hours of straight time or eight hours at time and a half.

The company felt originally that no remedy was justified. They argued that the entire concept of overtime payment is for work actually performed in excess of eight hours.

The Board supported the union's position. The Board ruled first the violation that occurred was not based on an interpretation of the language of the contract.

The violation was a deliberate change in the commitment made in 1958, which had been observed for the last 18 years.

It was determined "quite frequently" when Operation-Substation employees were in attendance during overhaul work, they did it on an overtime basis.

The union newsletter also contains a story on a retirees' association dinner and a report on an educational conference conducted by the union. Two-thirds of the back page is devoted to personal notes about members.

The union newsletter is semi-journalistic in style, as is the association's. Both report facts and are informal, even chatty, in personal notes about members.

Summary

For the practitioner who must communicate regularly with a membership of a specific public, large or small, the newsletter is efficient and inexpensive.

The position paper

For many years the position paper has been used by various organizations, especially religious groups, to tell their side of an issue; but it was the activist days of the 60s that brought it to the forefront.

The position paper is used to marshal arguments for or against an issue. It is distributed to group members to help them discuss the issue or even lobby for legislation.

The practitioner writes the paper for several reasons:

1. Some members don't have a comprehensive knowledge to argue an issue effectively;

2. Others don't have the time to research the subject;

3. In the case of lobbying a bill, there is a need for cogent arguments to influence the legislators.

149

In the position paper, the practitioner asks for an action to:

1. vote for an amendment
2. lobby a bill
3. change an attitude or an opinion

Argumentation style

Position papers are written like the persuasive brochure or position speech in the argumentation style. To write this way, you must develop a sense of the audience and anticipate their thoughts and feelings. You must express these attitudes in words familiar to them. What if you don't know who the audience might be? In that case, you must be doubly certain of your arguments and the facts.

Before writing, first ask youself:

What do you believe?
What are the specific arguments on your side of the issue?
Must you concede points?
Will the concessions hurt your side?

Then decide on the goal of your position paper:

1. To motivate a person to take an action of some kind? (Vote on an issue? Lobby a bill? Write a letter to the Editor?)
2. To have members of a public change their attitudes or opinions? (Why do they oppose your view? Are your arguments strong enough to influence them?)

There are several ways to start writing in argumentation style, as noted in Chapter 3 on brochures. Begin with a statement of fact, a premise, a question, or a sentence or two giving both sides of the issue.

What you want to do is give your organization's side of an issue clearly and forcefully. At the same time, you want to be sensitive to the audience, respectful of the other point of view. As such you must be diplomatic without weakening the force of your argument.

Remember that because the position paper is an aid to the members of your group, it must be easily read and understood. You should employ logic and control of syntax to persuade. Do not attempt to jolt the audience with a shocking word. Trying to persuade with a "one-shot" word seldom works. People react favorably to a well-written, concise, but comprehensive paper if the statements are logical, true, and fair.

Examples of argumentation

A group of homeowners are advocating the passage of a referendum in a state election. The group distributes its position paper to members, so they, in turn, can talk knowledgeably to friends and associates in promoting the passage of the referendum.

The group also plans to use the arguments in a neighborhood telephone campaign and as a basis for a radio talk show interview.

The proposed amendment to the state constitution is called *Property Classification for Tax Purposes*. Here's a summary of the amendment, as published by the newspaper:

> The legislature, under the proposed constitutional amendment, would be allowed to establish four different classes of property for tax purposes.
>
> Property in any one class would be assessed, rated and taxed proportionately. However, property in different classes could be rated and taxed differently.
>
> Reasonable exceptions could be granted by the legislature.
>
> All property, with the exceptions of wild lands, forest lands, and certain agricultural and horticultural lands, now is assessed and rated equally at full value for tax purposes, according to the constitution of this state.
>
> A vote in the affirmative (*yes*) would grant permission to the legislature to establish four classes of property that could be treated differently for tax purposes.
>
> A vote in the negative (*no*) would leave the constitution as it presently stands.

The homeowners advocating the passage of the referendum issued its members this position paper:

> A *yes* vote on Question One (the referendum) will stop the cities and towns from valuating property, especially homes, at 100 percent.
>
> Every city and town in the state must assess 100 percent valuation if the referendum does not pass.
>
> This statement means that residential property taxes (on homes and apartment buildings) will be increased $265 million throughout the state. Property taxes on insurance companies, real estate interests, commercial banks, and other big business will be cut by $265 million.

The elderly, who are among those least able to meet a tax increase, will be forced to pay taxes estimated at 700 percent more than before.

Nobody can blame the businesses for wanting a $265 cut in taxes.

But that $265 million increase in residential property taxes will have to be paid by the homeowner and the person who rents. They are not going to agree to that increase in taxes and rent.

A vote *yes* will stop 100 percent valuation. It will continue the practice of taxing homes less than business.

One hundred percent valuation will be enforced by a *no* vote. Residential property taxes will be increased by $265 million.

This position paper, advocating a *yes* vote, is short and to the point. It contains approximately 182 words, or a few more seconds than a minute radio commercial. It makes two specific points: the 100 percent valuation and the $265 million dollars. Each can be considered a very telling argument, especially for the property owner and for the person renting.

Naturally, another organization advocating a *no* vote on the referendum also issued a position paper to its members:

The legislature does not have a good record when it comes to making fair and sound tax decisions. In fact, a study of the past quarter of a century will show that the legislature leaves a lot to be desired.

The legislature does *not* have the right now to favor one class of property taxpayer over any other.

According to the constitution, all property must be taxed alike based on its real value.

If the voters approve the referendum, the protection we now enjoy, homeowners and businesspeople alike, will be lost.

If the legislature is given unlimited power, as suggested in this referendum, they will have the right to define and redefine property classes for tax purposes.

Members of the two houses will have the power to assign to each property class whatever rate of tax suits them.

Each year, the legislature could redefine property classes; there would be no time limit.

Equal treatment of all property must be continued. If it is not, the legislature will have both the businessperson and property owner at its mercy.

This position paper, with approximately 172 words, makes one specific point: do not let the legislature have the right of "unlimited power" to define and redefine property classes for tax purposes.

In comparison, note that both of these papers are concise; they are about the right length to be handed out and used by the members of their respective organizations. The writers used forceful arguments and reemphasized their points.

Activist training

Most people are not activists. They are not experienced in the techniques of public communication. Even armed with a position paper, many find it difficult to telephone people they don't know to discuss an issue. Thus you may find it to your organization's advantage to train members in persuasion.

Strategy of identification

A communicator must understand the strategy of identification. Successful politicians practice this technique by finding a common ground in which both they and the voter belong. They may both live in the same neighborhood, belong to the same union, attend the same church, have sons in Little League, or have mutual friends.

Identification strategy gives the communicator a way to establish the contact. Many people are wary of an invasion of their privacy even on the telephone.

In a door-to-door canvass of a neighborhood, select someone known to the residents. Make sure he does not call at meal time, late at night, or early in the morning. These suggestions may seem basic, but it is best that you mention them anyway to the members. That way you can reach the audience at the best time. Take into consideration the experience of one enthusiastic volunteer. She was met with a less than warm welcome from the male members of the neighborhood households on a Sunday afternoon in November. She was crestfallen; no one paid the slightest bit of attention to her arguments for a burning community issue.

What she later came to understand was that all the men were watching Sunday afternoon football on television!

Telephone campaigns

A new set of persuasion problems arise during a telephone campaign because phone volunteers make "cold" calls (the callers do not know the people they are telephoning).

In a telephone campaign, the caller must be natural, using conversational tones. He commits the position paper to memory: the arguments, statistics, even quotations, if any are being used. But he shouldn't read the paper; seldom is anyone convinced by someone reading a paper over the telephone. He must sound confident, competent in the field being discussed, knowledgeable, but not overbearing. This sense of confidence aids in persuading the listener the arguments presented are reliable and just.

The caller must be sensitive to the listener's attitude and the reasons for that attitude. At times, the listener's attitude is irrational, even inconsistent. The caller keeps his cool, despite the irrationality of the person. The caller shows respect for opposing views but returns the arguments for the other side. If he argues rationally without raising his voice, he might successfully persuade the listener.

Of course the caller tries to sound friendly, but it's best not to be too friendly, too intimate. Some inexperienced volunteers use the listener's first name in trying to create a warm atmosphere. Sometimes this works ("we are friends even if we don't know each other"), but it often backfires. Some people resent being called by their first name when they don't know the person telephoning.

Telephone volunteers must be flexible in their presentation. Each call represents a different set of circumstances; each situation must be dealt with accordingly. An experienced caller understands this fact and adjusts to it. He knows that if a listener is uninterested, he should bring forth his strongest argument to win attention and promote concern. If the listener is interested and can be persuaded or influenced, the caller draws his conclusions explicitly, repeating the main points of view. Liken the end of the conversation to a salesperson closing a sale by asking for an order.

Sensitivity. It cannot be overemphasized that the caller is always sensitive to the listener's attitudes and opinions, whether the discussion is on the telephone or in person. The communicator should use opposing views to his advantage, providing the opportunity for an open discussion.

Two or three versions

You will find it advantageous to write two or three versions of a position paper, or, at times, even a series of papers.

For example, a series might be necessary during a running controversy, in which new arguments or statistics are constantly being raised by both sides. The question of whether or not to legalize abortions is an illustration of this type of issue. In the late 60s and early 70s, religious groups, among others, waged a verbal war over the problem in public hearings, in the media (especially on talk shows on radio and television), and in discussion groups. Each side of the controversy (and the question continues to be debated) brought forth statistics and arguments as various bills were heard. Practitioners for organizations on both sides produced position papers on specific points of the question. There were, for example, various ideas on when the fetus actually becomes a human form. Physicians, biologists, and theologians all disagreed.

In another example, a practitioner might write a different position for each witness at a public hearing held by a legislative group on a proposed bill. In this case, each paper emphasizes one argument for or against the bill. It is pointless to have three witnesses repeat the same argument.

The practitioner chooses who presents which argument at the hearing. The best speaker is given the most telling argument. If the organization is a trade association, union, or association, usually the officers, the president, vice-president, or secretary testify. Most officers of a public organization are fairly articulate (this ability may be why they were elected); but there are some who have difficulty speaking in public, especially at a legislative hearing. A complicated position paper being presented by a person who has difficulty speaking in public can be a disaster. The practitioner would be unwittingly aiding the opposition!

Most legislators allow a person to read a prepared statement (the position paper) without interruption and then to file the paper with the committee. In case a legislator wants to question some of the statements, the speaker is supplied with back-up material. Many legislators are practicing attorneys, schooled in the techniques of cross-examination. As such, testifying can be a trying experience for the uninitiated. The back-up material comes in handy.

Fact sheet

For the more seasoned witness, a fact sheet is sufficient. It lists one- or two-sentence statements used by the witness to refresh his memory. Make sure to write each statement clearly and forcefully. The words must be correct in their denotations, and the sentence structure must mirror the statements' logic.

Summary

The practitioner writes a position paper to marshal arguments for or against an issue and distributes it to members of his client organization. The position paper always asks for an action, a vote, or a change in a person's opinion.

The complaint letter

No business or organization, however large or small, escapes complaints. Whether a chain of international hotels, a mom-and-pop restaurant, a university, a giant medical center, or a small community church, it is virtually impossible to satisfy everyone. There will always be a dissatisfied customer, patient, student, client, alumnus, or parishioner. This unhappy person usually vents his anger with a letter to the president.

Customer complaints are increasing. No one is sure why, but it is true that today is the age of consumer advocacy.

Most large organizations, automobile manufacturers, airlines, department stores, and retail chains have customer relations departments. Their responsibility is to work out each problem with the customer. These companies have a set of guidelines that cover the majority of complaints encountered.

An example would be the complaint of the airline passenger with a damaged suitcase. "Please have it repaired and send us the bill" is the traditional airline answer, assuming the necessary forms have been filled out and the claim is legitimate. This method of dealing with complaints uses the information gathered throughout the years on various patterns of major complaint areas.

You might well ask, "Wouldn't it be easier to change the pattern causing the problem?" The answer is *yes*. Many times a complaint reveals the seed of a growing problem that can be easily dealt with in the embryonic stage. If ignored over years, the problem becomes difficult to solve.

There are times when a problem must continue. In this case it cannot be resolved because of unusual circumstances. Or there may be valid reason not to change the problem despite continued complaints.

Guidelines

The larger the organization, the more complaints. The answers to complaints must be uniform as the number increases.

As the practitioner, you will need to write a series of answering letters to common complaints to be used solely as a guide. Each actual letter is then changed and/or adjusted to meet the charge by the customer.

Each letter received is promptly answered, or at least acknowledged, no matter how vitriolic or petty. Make sure that each complaint letter is handled on an individual basis and not answered by a form letter. A form letter's impersonalness can cause additional problems.

Sometimes a simple "Thank you for your letter and bringing this matter to our attention" will resolve the problem. The fact that an officer of the organization answered is sufficient to the customer.

Policy

Policy and procedures must be spelled out, and they must be adhered to within reason. A practitioner with the responsibility of customer/client complaints works out a reasonable policy with management covering all complaint areas.

Manual

When more than two or three employees handle complaints, company policy on certain procedures is written in a formal complaint manual. Loose-leaf notebooks are used by many departments, so the pages can be interchanged or substituted.

Often when an established company policy is changed, a new set of complaints are encountered. Establishment of policy is a management function, but an alert practitioner anticipates the public's attitude and suggests strategy to combat possible problems.

Chronic complainer

The chronic complainer is not unusual. There are those who delight in challenging a certain organization on a week-to-week or month-to-month basis. Once these "chronics" find a name (usually the president of the organization), they take great delight in dashing off irate letters on some inconsequential matter.

Psychologists recommend ignoring the writer when it is apparent that it is impossible to satisfy him. They point out that this type of complainer, the continual letter writer, seeks attention. The barrage of letters will end when letters are not answered or answered with a simple acknowledgment.

Fortunately or unfortunately, practitioners schooled in attempting at all times to resolve all problems, no matter how minor, answer each letter.

For example, one religious group engaged in the battle for race equality during the 60s received a series of letters. While many of the letters the Bishop received praised the church's stand, others said that the church had no right to be involved.

The Bishop answered each letter carefully, writing the reasons for the church's philosophy and his own conviction in the matter. One communicant was adamant, repeating in letter after letter the same complaint, that the church did not belong in the civil rights movement. The Bishop, with the patience of Job, again explained the church's position and the reasons for it.

Summer came and the Bishop was on vacation for a month. The communicant's weekly complaint letter arrived. A summer public relations intern was alone in the public relations department and the letter found its way to the intern.

The intern answered:

Dear ——:

Thank you for your letter.

Sincerely,

The Public Relations Department

The communicant never wrote again.

Valid complaint letters

Consider valid complaint letters in a serious light. The customer feels quite deeply about an incident or experience, even if the complaint subject is common.

A case in point: An executive flying from Chicago to Los Angeles on an early evening flight was not served dinner. There had been an incorrect passenger count and the attendant was one dinner short. The attendant thought it funny that the executive was served a less-than-adequate meal of tea sandwiches and a cup of coffee. Laughing, he spilled coffee on the passenger's lap. Naturally the executive wrote a complaint letter, spelling out the details. He was not angry; he wrote that he could see the humor, but not at the expense of having coffee spilled over him.

Several days later, the executive received a neatly typed letter saying he would receive a check for the value of the missed meal. The letter ended, "Thank you for flying ——." There was no apology for the missed meal or spilled coffee. The tone of the letter was business-like, giving the impression, "You'll get your money back, what else do you want?"

The executive then wrote to the president of the airline, outlining the details and enclosing a copy of the letter he received in answer to his original complaint.

The president made immediate amends to the executive; but what is interesting about this anecdote is the subsequent change in company policy. The president asked that in the future the vice-president in charge of public relations review each letter answering a complaint, especially in regard to the letter's tone.

Many new members of a customer relations department find it difficult to write an answer to a complaint letter. Because they may feel inhibited, they may respond sounding cold and unfriendly. To overcome this feeling, they may become too jocular. Both extremes do little to resolve the problem. Taking a hint from the previous example, it's a good idea to allow an experienced person, preferably one with public relations sensitivity, to review each answer to a complaint.

Sometimes when reading a complaint letter, it's hard to take it seriously if the letter is not well written (words misspelled, bad grammar, etc.). Remember that even though a letter is written in a clumsy manner, the complaint still may be important.

Examples of complaints and responses

These complaints were received in the corporate office of a national corporation for a chain of franchised figure salons.

Last year, I went to —— as the guest of a friend. Before we began the exercises I was taken into an office where I was pressured into signing up for $25.

A few days after the exercises, I suffered great pain in my legs and back and I realized that because of my past health history this was not for me.

I wrote a letter and asked for my money back and they told me I would be an open file and could begin a six-week course at a later date, but no refund of the money.

Last night I received a call from the —— salon asking when I would be coming in. I told them it would only be damaging to me if I came in and that I would like my $25 back. The reply was we would like to have it in writing and it's too late for that now. I replied that I did send a letter and she told me I had special forms to fill out and that it was too late. I told her I was never told of a special form and that it would seem to me this should have been told at the time they were signing me up. Her answer was 'well it's too late anyway.'

I have not attended one class and you have had my money almost for a year. You've made money on my interest. Forget the interest and mail me my check and I will be very appreciative. Otherwise I will have to report the high pressure to the comsumer protection agency.

I am sure there has been a misunderstanding, and I hope this can be cleared up.

Thank you for your time. I will look forward to hearing from you.

The reply:

Dear Mrs. ——:

We are truly sorry for your unfortunate experience at our salon in ——.

We are enclosing a check for $25 and we appreciate your patience and your sense of fair play.

Very truly yours,

The Customer Relations Department

In answering this complaint, the essential thing was the refund of the money and a sincere apology, along with an appreciation of the person's patience and fair play. To write a lengthy explanation of why the money was not refunded at once would only add to the woman's frustration.
Another type of complaint:

I am an annual member in my third year. I used to go to the ——, but since the new one in —— opened I got transferred there as it is nearer for me where I live.

To get to the point, I am complaining of the temperature being too warm for a person doing exercise. The people find this true but no one has taken it further other than just saying its hot.

Sixty-five degrees is a bit too warm for people doing exercises, but naturally cold for the help, especially the owner as she sits in her office. I have complained many times and get nowhere so I thought I would take the matter up with you.

Would you kindly be concerned and see what a better temperature we could all have to do our exercises in.

The reply:

Thank you for calling our attention to the problem with the temperature at the ——. We have discussed the problem at length with the franchise owner.

She has told us she is fully aware of the problem and that the air conditioning unit is at fault. During these hot months, the unit will not cool the salon below the 65-degree mark.

A new air conditioning unit has been ordered and is scheduled for installation within the next three weeks.

Until that time, three portable units will be used in an effort to reduce the temperature to the 60-degree level. We hope this will work and our members will be able to exercise in comfort.

Again, thank you for your patience. We appreciate your letter to us. You are a valued member at the —— salon.

Another type of complaint:

The week of March 16 I sent a letter to your —— salon about my membership. I stated in the letter that I signed up for three months' ending April 4, and due to a back injury I was unable to attend exercises since the end of January or beginning of February. I want to know if I could get an extension and I haven't heard from them as of this date. I am also pregnant and if I continue the program I will have to do so soon. I would appreciate an answer as soon as possible.

The reply:

Thank you for your letter. You certainly may have an extension to complete your program.

We are sorry the salon owner did not answer your letter promptly. Your original letter to the salon was misplaced and never answered. The owner is sorry for the inconvenience.

After your baby is born and when your doctor feels it is safe for you to exercise, we would like you to have another program of three months as a guest of the company.

This is our way of saying thank you for your interest in ——, and congratulations.

A fourth complaint letter:

I am a member of the —— salon, and I wish to complain about the staff. No one pays any attention to me and they pay attention to all the other members.

Last week I walked into the salon and asked ——, a technician, if she would show me how to do an exercise. She said she would and never did. I told the manager about ——, and she said she would ask her about it. I then told the owner.

Would you speak to the staff about paying me some attention?

The reply:

Thank you for your letter. You're a valued member and we're sorry you feel you're not getting the attention from our staff of technicians.

The one thing we stress in our continual training program is service, and when a valued member complains about lack of service, we check into it right away.

We have talked to each member of the staff and found that in the past week, the technicians were busy and unable to devote as much time to members as they wished.

There were a number of new members who needed instruction on their beginning exercises and the technician to whom you spoke was unable to get back to you before you left.

We realize the problem and the owner of the salon is putting additional staff members on this week to take care of the new members.

Again, we're sorry for the problem and we hope it is now resolved.

We certainly appreciate the time you took to bring this to our attention. As we said before, you are a valued member.

The complaint, it was found on investigation, was not really legitimate because the member wanted constant attention. However, it was decided to answer the letter apologetically, but not blaming the technician. Some explanations were made (the staff was helping new members) and some solutions were offered (hiring of additional staff).

Any service organization (bank, restaurant, hospital) is always concerned about how their employees treat those they serve. Most of these organizations, restaurant chains especially, supply cards, usually at the cashier's desk, on which customers can comment on the food or the service. These cards, pre-addressed to the company's headquarters with the postage prepaid, are headed: *Comments* or *Complaints-Compliments*. Their opening paragraph reads:

Your satisfaction with our food and service is important to us. Would you take a minute and answer these questions? Just circle your answer and drop this card into the mail.

How did you like our service?
excellent, good, fair, poor

How do you like our menu?
excellent, good, fair, poor

How would you improve our service?

_____

_____

Restaurant complaints

Restaurant complaints fall into three broad categories: poor service, cold or badly prepared food, or being ignored by the order clerk.

If the complaint is mild ("We waited ten minutes for our soup, then it was cold"), you would simply apologize. If (*only if*) there is a legitimate reason for the delay, a problem over which management has little or no control, then you can mention an excuse.

Restaurants win approval based on these three basic factors: cuisine, decor, and the personality of the staff. If any of these three factors break down for any length of time, a restaurant or even a restaurant chain seldom survives.

Customers don't usually complain about price. If the customer feels the restaurant charges too much or does not receive value, he just does not return.

Litigation

If you receive a letter serious enough to warrant litigation, turn it over to the legal department or to the insurance company. You might acknowledge the letter, but leave the answer to someone else.

Technical

Sometimes complaints of a technical nature require an answer by a professional in that specific field.

Hospitals face this problem. For example, a patient or the relative of a patient may complain about a certain technique or therapy, or say that there is a lack of adequate care. This kind of complaint (the questioning of professional judgment or competence) could end in a malpractice suit. In this case, let the answer be reviewed by the hospital's legal counsel. Even if there is *no* threat of suit, it's best to let the medical department answer the letter.

Hospital practitioners can answer such complaints as why visitors are not allowed in intensive care units or why there is a long delay in being seen in a clinic. In the following letter, a practitioner responds to a new patient who waited two hours before being helped.

Thank you for your letter describing the events of your recent visit to our medical clinic.

It is unfortunate that there was a long wait, but we feel that if we explain the procedure it might help you to understand the reason for the wait to see the doctor.

As a new patient, you did not have a specific appointment, nor did we have your medical history. This is why you first had an interview with one of our admitting clerks.

You were then given a series of routine blood and urine tests, so that the physician might better evaluate your respective condition. The doctor assigned to your case had three scheduled appointments before he was able to see you. Naturally, the physician takes as much time with each patient as he feels is necessary.

The doctor saw you after his three scheduled appointments. We attempt to have all our patients seen as fast as possible. That is why we schedule appointments for patients.

You will note that you have a specific time to be seen by the doctor for your next visit to the clinic. You will not have to wait the next time unless there is an emergency.

We hope this letter answers your questions about our clinic procedure and we appreciate the opportunity to write to you.

There are some administrators and staff personnel who would say that such a complaint is a crank letter and that as such, should not be answered. The practitioner, however, felt that it should be answered with an explanation of why new clinic patients experience delays in seeing a physician. After seeing several letters of this type, the practitioner wrote a brochure that was given to all new clinic patients. The brochure explained the medical clinic procedure step by step so that the new patients understood the reasons for delays.

Handling complaints

Each industry handles complaints differently. The nature of the business dictates to a great extent how a complaint is processed and by whom.

You may be asked not only to answer the customer but also to investigate the circumstances. For example, you might receive a complaint claiming that an employee was rude. You would talk to everyone involved to see if the customer really was insulted. Because you're not an experienced investigator, you may be tense when questioning this particular employee. Your uneasiness could cause the employee to be on the defensive, so make sure to show empathy at the start. A display of understanding works and you'll get a fairly accurate description of what happened. The practitioner who opens with, "This customer says you swore at her. Did you?" will not get far. Instead of accusing, put the employee at ease in an honest attempt to find out the truth: "I know there are two sides and I certainly want to hear your side."

If both customer and employee are equally at fault, your answering letter shouldn't blame anyone. Instead, ignore altogether the specifics of the incident.

Here's a sample letter:

> Thank you for your letter and giving your side of this unfortunate incident. You are a valued customer and when a episode like this occurs, we are upset.
>
> We certainly hope this will not prevent you from coming into our store and continuing your patronage.
>
> Again, thank you for writing. We appreciate it.

In this way, neither the employee nor the customer is blamed.

Although at one time the adage, "The customer is always right," was the rule, do not try to keep the customer happy at the expense of an innocent employee.

The fund-raising letter

Public relations practitioners are not fund-raisers per se. Many do work for nonprofit organizations and institutions, but their responsibility is communications, not fund raising.

Instead, professional fund-raisers are hired for capital gifts campaigns or when a group seeks funds throughout the year. Practitioners write and produce the fund-raising brochures and letters for these professionals.

Often the fund-raising letter is used by hospitals, schools, churches, youth groups, half-way houses, associations for the elderly, and a host of others. A letter creates a personal contact; it can be personalized. In the case of a special fund-raising campaign, it can be made personal to the point of being confidential. Also, whereas a message in a newspaper or magazine competes for the reader's attention with other ads or articles, a letter does not.

169

Write the letter to fit the objective of the institution: an annual donation, a deferred-giving program, or a capital gift. In it you will try to persuade the reader that your organization is worthy of a gift. You may want to use the identification technique by mentioning the reader's connection with the organization: resident of the community, alumnus, parent, former patient, relative of someone who benefitted from the service, etc.

Cold letters and mailing lists

At one time solicitation letters were used by literally thousands of nonprofit groups. But due to today's high cost of producing and mailing, cold letters are not sent out as much as before.

Institutions often maintain lists of those who have given previously or those who might be potential donors for other reasons. Obviously it's more likely to get a return from someone shown to be willing to help the institution operate.

Format and timing

Fund raisers agree two factors are important in a letter campaign: the letter's format (content and layout); and the timing of the request.

Never try to solicit around tax time, April 15, although you may send letters before the end of the year to remind donors that their gift is tax deductible.

Religious holidays such as Christmas and Easter are sometimes used for annual solicitation drives. Colleges take advantage of class anniversaries, especially the twenty-fifth, to raise funds.

Prewriting considerations

Before you begin writing, consider how you are going to mail the letters, what your production schedule will be, if there is to be any additional material with the letter (return envelope, pledge card), what stationery design you'll use, and who will sign the letter.

Mailing

A number of years ago hospitals included a self-addressed stamped envelope. Volunteers painstakingly moistened and placed the stamps on literally thousands of envelopes. With the cost of postage today, very few organizations can afford putting stamps on return envelopes. However, some fund raisers still feel a self-addressed envelope is worth the cost and include it with the letter.

Many groups including postage with their return envelopes use mailing permits; this strategy means they pay postage costs only on actual returns. Other organizations put in a self-addressed envelope without postage, hoping that the donor will want to buy a stamp to send in the donation.

Stationery design

There is no rule about what to print on the stationery. You should decide how best to portray your organization to its constituency. Many practitioners use the regular stationery of the organization, which has printed on it the names of the officers and trustees.

Each name lends a sense of credibility to the work of the group. The reason the person is on the board is that he occupies a position of some prominence in the community or in his field. But a few prominent people lend their names without really knowing the group's actual work or how well they serve a need or community. Remember that the most sophisticated philanthropists pay little heed to the names on a letterhead; instead, they study the actual work of the group. You may wish to create a letterhead using photos and drawings illustrating your group's work.

Signature

Who signs the letter? Generally, the president signs. He usually is a person of prominence, well known and respected. One of his responsibilities as the head of a group is to lend his name to fund-raising communications.

Staff of the fund committee, including you and the fund-raiser, do not sign such letters. Some volunteers, if well known, may sign letters to friends.

Here's an example. The chief of the medical staff of Mercy Hospital signed an annual fund-raising letter for nearly thirty years. Most respected, the physician's name was synonymous with the hospital's service to the community. Because more than 100 letters were sent in the annual drive, a facsimile of his signature was used. The signature, printed in blue, looked hand signed. The printer charged extra for this second color (in addition to black), but the blue ink facsimile stood out and was worth it.

During special gift campaigns for Mercy, the president and board members wrote individual letters to friends, associates, and relatives. Whereas some members preferred that the practitioner outline or write the letter, some wanted to write their own letters without any help or even suggestions. The board president, for example, who was also the head of a bank, wrote fifty letters to friends and associates in longhand. The response was generous.

Production

Style

Naturally your purpose for writing will determine your writing style. For example:

1. *Argumentation*—why the institution is important to the community

2. *Description*—used by organizations caring for the chronically ill, elderly, orphaned

3. *Narration*—listing the accomplishments of the organization

Various techniques can be used. Some letters use headlines:

Your College Needs Funds Now!
There Will Be a New Science
  Building on Campus Next Year
We Can Cure Cancer Now If......

Others use a personal technique:

Dear Frank:
  Our class has a unique opportunity to be of a real service to the school.

What technique you employ depends on the nature of the drive and the recipient of the letter. If the letter is being sent to a carefully selected few, it would be personalized and probably hand signed. But if the letter is being sent to a thousand class members, it would be generalized:

Dear Member of the Class of 1955:

Length

People disagree about how long the letter should be. While copywriters for print and broadcast make their selling message concise, direct-mail copywriters take two, three, or even four pages to sell their product or service.

The origin of the time-honored copywriting formula—attention, interest, desire, and action—is from the direct-mail writing fraternity. This formula, AIDA, may be applied to the fund-raising letter:

1. Capture attention.

2. Create an interest.

3. Produce a desire to resolve a problem, do a good deed.

4. Ask for an action: send a check, make a commitment, sign a pledge card.

The letter doesn't have the space limitations of a brochure. Instead it gives you as much room as you need to persuade the reader. You may need a page and a half, or three concise, well-written paragraphs.

Try to sense when you've written too much or too little. It's possible to spoil the message by putting in too many details of little interest or too little detail to do an adequate "selling" job.

After you write the annual solicitation letter, have it typed and reproduced. Individually add the name of the recipient. Some automatic typewriters can add each name at the start and in the body of the letter. Many organizations computerize their mailing lists. Some make sure that only certain types of letters are sent out to recipients, depending on their past giving patterns.

Type

Choose a readable typeface and make sure that the reproduction is clear and crisp. There is an old adage in producing fund-raising literature: "A reader's disposition to give generously relates positively to his ability to see well."

Examples

This letter from a religious group, sent to 50,000 families, was mailed out in the Christmas season. Included was a self-addressed envelope without stamp or mailing permit.

> Dear Member:
>
> *Emergency* is the key word in the use of the Christmas appeal funds by the Department of Social Relations.
>
> No one should have to go hungry in this country, nor be unclothed with no place to sleep. Yet in this city alone there are 5,000 unattached, homeless men, largely alcoholics.
>
> All through the year—winter, spring, summer, and fall—the hungry, partially naked, and homeless appeal to the clergy for help. Often this help is sought on weekends when welfare agencies are closed.
>
> And it can vary from just one meal to a room overnight, to a change of clothing, to a used bed for a child without anything to sleep on.
>
> Requests come from all directions. One public defender told us about a sixteen-year-old runaway who is in a local detention center. She needs a temporary home for eight weeks before a permanent plan can be put into operation for her care. She was picked up for stealing a basket of fruit.
>
> An old man came to us. He had fallen and his clothes were caked with dirt and blood. He asked if we had a change of clothing.
>
> We saw a young refugee with psychotic tendencies who cannot hold a job longer than a few weeks. Could he be helped to get his shoes from the repairshop?
>
> A mother's relief check was fully used by unusual demands this period—a food order would keep her family eating the next few days.
>
> The Bishop referred to us a young student from Kenya who needs money and a job to finish his college work this semester.
>
> So the emergencies come to us daily and always there is the urgency for immediate help.
>
> This Christmas appeal is the only source of aid for these purposes. Its funds meet these needs 365 days a year.
>
> Please make out your check and send it to us today in the enclosed envelope. God will bless you.

The letter was written by the clergyman heading the Social Service Department. There was no committee, and the Bishop, who conducted the fund drive, was his immediate superior.

Another example is a letter to all 100,000 alumni members of a university. This campaign was in addition to the annual class solicitation. The focus was more on tax reduction than on loyalty to the alma mater.

Dear Alumnus:

Many of our alumni have requested the university to set up a deferred giving program. Such a program is now in existence to encourage giving through life income trusts, annuities, and bequests.

Not only does the university benefit by such gifts, but the alumnus receives significant tax advantages.

The university is prepared to give you additional information in confidence and without obligation. There is a card enclosed for your convenience.

The enclosed *Personal Information Record Booklet* will assist you. And in the event that you have already provided for the university in your will, notice of that on the enclosed *confidential* card would be appreciated.

Your university urges your consideration of this productive way of giving.

Included with the letter was a card addressed to the Alumni Deferred Giving Committee, with a printed mailing permit.

On the message side of the card was printed:

I am interested in the benefits and tax-saving opportunities through deferred gifts to the university.

Please send me information on:
   Life income trusts
   University annuities
   Including the university in my will

The message side also included blanks for the alumnus' name, address, and class, as well as two blanks for comments.

The next letter in this campaign by the university read:

Dear Alumnus:

The response from the *Personal Information Record Booklet* mailing was excellent. As a result, we are enclosing another booklet, *What You Should Know about Your Will.*

Many alumni have benefitted through tax savings realized by gifts of life income trust and annuity.

Through such gifts, an individual can contribute property to the university but reserve the income for his or her life and the life of the beneficiary.

MIAMI UNIVERSITY
OXFORD, OHIO

THE MIAMI UNIVERSITY FUND

December, 1978

NEVER GIVE UP.

When Winston Churchill was an old, old man, retired, rheumatic, rarely seen in public, the officials of his old school invited him to give a chapel talk to all the boys.

He agreed.

The Chapel was full for the occasion. The faculty all turned out, too. The townspeople, as well. Even a few reporters stood poised around the edges.

The Great Man was introduced and the crowd settled back in their chairs and benches for the chapel hour.

Churchill arose, cleared his throat, peered around the hall, and then, without preliminary, growled slowly:

"Never Give Up. Never.   Never.   Never.   ...   Never!"

...and sat down.

Churchill spoke, and wrote, billions of words, but I've taken those seven as my guide for writing you just once more this year about the 1978 Miami University Fund. This is surely my last chance; the calendar will take care of that.

Your contribution last year, along with the thousands of others received during 1977, has made your university a Better Miami... you can be truly proud. But, as I write this letter, our records don't show a contribution from you during 1978.

We may have received your check before this reminder arrives, but the Churchill words would haunt me if I gave up too soon. So if you have not already sent it, won't you mail your check for 1978 now? It's never too late - Never. Never. Never.

...Never! - unless it's after December 31st.

John E. Dolibois
Vice President

JED/pb

Courtesy of Miami University.

Figure 12–1. These fund-raising letters use imaginative anecdotes and interesting headlines to involve the reader. Notice the stationery designs.

the **annual program** of THE MIAMI UNIVERSITY FUND

OXFORD, OHIO 45056

Projects for 1979:
Scholarships and Student Aid
The University Library
Environmental Sciences
International Studies Programs
Sesquicentennial Chapel
Miami University Student Foundation
Cultural Enrichment and Other Activities
Academic Advancement
Undergraduate and Graduate Research
Alumni Weekend
Alumni and Development Activities

April, 1979

WANT TO WIN
EVERY TIME??

A friend of mine, in Las Vegas recently on an educational visit, noticed an elderly woman feeding dollars into a machine and scooping out the change clattering down,

... every time she pulled the handle.

Sniffing an educational experience, he moved in closer to catch the secret, then left rather quickly.

He didn't want to be nearby when the lady finally discovered she was playing the machine that dishes out change for silver dollars.

Actually, that was probably not such a bad idea. By breaking even she was clearly doing much better at Las Vegas than most visitors. But I'm writing, of course, about a far better deal. When you bet your dollars on The Miami University Fund you do much better than break even.

... you win every time.

Your gifts, combined with others, do really great things. For years they've added an extra dimension that sets your favorite university apart from other state assisted schools. Whether you designate your contribution for scholarships, library support, or any other project listed in the enclosed folder, it pays off big for students, for faculty and for Miami itself. And, because you reap the satisfaction of knowing that good things happen, you win, too.

However, even the surest of bets must be placed. And, for 1979, it's possible that now is the best time. Any gift, at any time and in any size, helps build up the Fund jackpot, but the ones that blossom in the spring work harder, longer. So think about action now, won't you ...

You can't beat the odds.

John E. Dolibois

JED/dgi

John E. Dolibois
Vice President

 many gifts combine to do great things for Miami

Several such gifts have been received, and in each case, the alumnus was amazed at the substantial tax savings.

More information is available on how you may benefit the university and realize substantial tax savings. Please return the enclosed *confidential* card.

The card enclosed in the letter with the booklet was similar to the card mailed before.

Realize that these letters are examples and must not be used as guidelines. Deferred giving and annuity programs have many legal ramifications. All promotional copy must be referred to legal counsel before being printed and distributed. Because tax laws change frequently, all letters promising tax benefits must be reviewed and approved by counsel.

Summary

Practitioners write fund-raising letters for nonprofit organizations and institutions. The letter creates a personal contact; its goal is to persuade the reader that the organization is worthy of a gift.

Index